NEW DIRECTIONS FOR ADULT AND CONTINUING EDUCATION

Susan Imel, *Ohio State University*
Ralph G. Brockett, *University of Tennessee, Knoxville*
EDITORS-IN-CHIEF

Assessing Adult Learning in Diverse Settings: Current Issues and Approaches

Amy D. Rose
Northern Illinois University

Meredyth A. Leahy
Regents College

EDITORS

Number 75, Fall 1997

JOSSEY-BASS PUBLISHERS
San Francisco

ASSESSING ADULT LEARNING IN DIVERSE SETTINGS: CURRENT ISSUES AND
APPROACHES
Amy D. Rose, Meredyth A. Leahy (eds.)
New Directions for Adult and Continuing Education, no. 75
Susan Imel, Ralph G. Brockett, Editors-in-Chief

Microfilm copies of issues and articles are available in 16mm and 35mm,
as well as microfiche in 105mm, through University Microfilms Inc., 300
North Zeeb Road, Ann Arbor, Michigan 48106–1346.

ISSN 1052-2891   ISBN 0-7879-9840-0

NEW DIRECTIONS FOR ADULT AND CONTINUING EDUCATION is part of The
Jossey-Bass Higher and Adult Education Series and is published quarterly
by Jossey-Bass Inc., Publishers, 350 Sansome Street, San Francisco, California 94104–1342. Periodicals postage paid at San Francisco, California,
and at additional mailing offices. Postmaster: Send address changes to
New Directions for Adult and Continuing Education, Jossey-Bass Inc.,
Publishers, 350 Sansome Street, San Francisco, California 94104–1342.

SUBSCRIPTIONS cost $54.00 for individuals and $90.00 for institutions,
agencies, and libraries.

EDITORIAL CORRESPONDENCE should be sent to the Editor-in-Chief,
Susan Imel, ERIC/ACVE, 1900 Kenny Road, Columbus, Ohio 43210–1090.
E-mail: imel.1@osu.edu.

Cover photograph by Wernher Krutein/PHOTOVAULT © 1990.

Jossey-Bass Web address: http://www.josseybass.com

Printed in the United States of America on acid-free recycled paper con-
taining 100 percent recovered waste paper, of which at least 20 percent is
postconsumer waste.

CONTENTS

Editors' Notes

In this era of greater accountability, assessment has taken on great urgency within all levels of education. Adult education, because of its marginal status within traditional educational institutions, is vulnerable. At the same time, business and industry, particularly with the advent of the learning organization, have integrated continuous cycles of learning and education into the everyday work life of individuals at all levels of corporate and industrial life. As assessment and evaluation emerge as central concerns within adult education, important issues remain unresolved. The purpose of this volume is to examine assessment approaches analytically from a variety of programmatic levels and to look at the implications of these differing approaches.

It would seem that the central issues facing adult educators concerned with assessment are obvious. The essential question is, *What do people learn in programs?* Additionally, we can ask, *Do individuals learn what is being taught?* Of course, the simplest and most straightforward way to measure this learning is through testing, before and after the program. Not only does testing show the "value added" to the individual by the program, but it also measures individual progress and shows overall program effectiveness. As these chapters show, however, the dimensions of assessment are far more complex than these rather simplistic questions can address. Assessment involves much more than simply measuring the results of classroom interaction. It must take into account a multiplicity of stakeholders and their understanding of the kinds of learning that occur. In addition, measuring in this rather standard way can limit understanding of the kinds of learning that are actually taking place. What about unanticipated experiences or affective changes? How does one measure transformative experiences, which may not incrementally add to a knowledge base but which may fundamentally change how individuals view themselves and their world?

The very complexity of the adult's life makes measurement and assessment a difficult task. In addition, adults approach each learning opportunity with a vast reservoir of experience that can both enhance and hinder the learning experience. The cultural biases that inhibit true assessment of children's learning are magnified in the assessment of adults. Additionally, assessment of adult learning is really three-pronged: one aspect measures the educational experience, another looks at how this learning is actually transferred into the everyday settings of individuals, and the third examines what people bring into any given educational experience, in order either to place them appropriately or to accredit them increasingly in some way for this ex-mural learning.

In the opening chapter, Carol E. Kasworm and Catherine A. Marienau identify some general principles for the assessment of adult learning. Focusing primarily on outcomes assessment, they draw from a diverse body of programmatic literature in developing basic premises of adult learning and connecting these premises to good assessment practice.

In Chapter Two, Stephen D. Brookfield examines the complexities of assessing critical thinking. Admitting that critical thinking is a skill that is deeply embedded within individual contexts, Brookfield identifies exercises designed to recognize growth or change while also helping individuals to reflect on their own experiences and on their sense of these experiences.

The next three chapters examine different ways in which educators recognize and evaluate adults' prior learning experiences. In Chapter Three, Richard J. Hamilton details the processes by which the Program on Non-collegiate Sponsored Instruction (PONSI) evaluates the training programs of business, industry, and professional groups and makes credit recommendations to colleges and universities. Building on the World War II experiences of the American Council on Education (ACE) in evaluating the military training of veterans, PONSI evaluations provide adults with the opportunity to have their work-related training programs formally recognized by academic institutions.

In Chapter Four, Elana Michelson goes beyond the programmatic approach of PONSI to examine the portfolio process. Michelson is particularly concerned with the narrowness of efforts that seek to identify students' generalizable knowledge while eschewing the context within which this learning has developed. She points to the inherent cultural biases that permeate a process that has emphasized its objectivity in order to gain acceptance within the academy.

In Chapter Five, Paula E. Peinovich, Mitchell S. Nesler, and Todd S. Thomas discuss how Regents College has incorporated an outcomes assessment approach into a full-fledged collegiate program. Rather than relying on assessments of learning gained only through formal study, Regents College utilizes diverse modalities to incorporate prior learning into degree programs. These modalities include standardized examinations, PONSI evaluations, and portfolio development.

The final three chapters move beyond higher education to explore assessment issues and approaches in other contexts. In Chapter Six, Eunice N. Askov, Barbara L. Van Horn, and Priscilla S. Carman describe strategies useful in assessing learning in adult basic education. They note the issues that educators face in assessing learning in this area, and go on to enumerate the strategies used by educators to overcome the fears of this population while simultaneously dealing with external demands for greater accountability.

In Chapter Seven, Patricia L. Inman and Sally Vernon describe the ways in which business and industry are introducing the idea of continuous learning into the workplace, and how this idea has led to the development of some innovative approaches to assessment, thus affecting both how the new learning can be assessed and how it has been utilized. Of particular importance is the current emphasis on reflection and self-assessment as the keys to effective learning within this particular context.

In Chapter Eight, Judith M. Ottoson expands the very idea of assessment. Noting that assessment of training often entails an examination of how new skills are integrated into the workplace and other areas of life, she develops several different lenses through which this issue of transfer can be understood. These lenses have implications for many different areas of adult education.

The issues raised in these chapters are explored in the final summary chapter. Suggestions for future directions are discussed in the conclusion.

Amy D. Rose
Meredyth A. Leahy
Editors

AMY D. ROSE is associate professor of adult continuing education at Northern Illinois University, DeKalb.

MEREDYTH A. LEAHY is dean of liberal arts at Regents College of the University of the State of New York, Albany.

Principles to guide adult-oriented assessment are offered in this chapter along with illustrations of good practice from higher education and other sectors providing education for adults.

Principles for Assessment of Adult Learning

Carol E. Kasworm, Catherine A. Marienau

The landscape of adult learning assessment reflects a complex geography of diverse terrains and climates. In particular, key sectors of our society—most notably education, business, and increasingly, professional associations and related arenas of professional practice—recognize the importance of assessment. These entities see assessment as guiding educational efforts as well as helping to clarify outcomes and benefits for learners, organizations, and the larger society.

Higher education has provided key leadership in creating and critically examining varied assessment schemes and strategies. This turn toward assessment is being stimulated by new accreditation standards that require articulation of outcomes and heightened institutional accountability, often tied to state funding mandates.

Various organizations in other arenas are also tending the assessment landscape. Businesses are increasingly pressured to identify and assess the essential skills, knowledge, and attributes required of their employees. The future viability and competitive edge of many companies depend on creating a knowledgeable and skilled workforce, as well as providing leadership for continuously upgrading the knowledge of their employees in rapidly changing environments. Professional associations and related continuing professional education programs are also encouraging continuous learning in order to meet the rising standards of performance dictated by advances in technology and knowledge.

The authors wish to thank Morris Fiddler, School for New Learning, DePaul University, for his assistance in final preparation of this manuscript.

The assessment process must address learning on multiple levels—perception, action, and critical reflection—and from multiple perspectives—those of the learner, the instructional program, and the various contexts of adult life. Thus the assessment of adult learning reflects "ecological validity." This concept aligns assessment with *content* (knowledge, skills, and attitudes), *context* (authentic activity in relation to the culture of learning and communities of practice), *learner* (characteristics, history, goals, and interrelationships), and *instructional practice* (strategies, goals, and actions that provide self-referencing assessment and focus on situated learning environments to bring the significance of real-life contexts into the learning process) (Choi and Hannafin, 1995; Young, 1993). This chapter offers five key principles of assessment derived from common premises of adult learning. Each principle is presented with illustrations of assessment practices in different areas.

Creating a Space for Adult Learners in Assessment

The complex lives of adults and their varied patterns of participation in learning challenge traditional assessment practices. In spite of their growing prominence in colleges and universities, adult learners typically are ignored in the strategies that inform most collegiate institutional assessment programs (Banta, 1993; Spille, 1993). Current institutional assessment programs are typically based on the characteristics of young adult learners, and tend to assume linear, continuous participation oriented to a residential academic learning community. Even within the adult higher education community, adult-oriented assessment activities are still somewhat limited. Assessment practices tend to be derivations of those that faculty have applied to younger students, and reiterations of those they themselves experienced as students.

The nature of adult participation and the complexity of adult students' lives challenge the historic assessment frameworks of higher education. Adult learners usually do not study on a full-time basis. Rather, they enter or reenter college anywhere and anytime between their mid-twenties and their seventies. They are likely to have attended two or three other institutions of higher learning, as well as to have participated in varied instructional delivery systems. These adults bring a rich tapestry of past schooling, formal learning through work or community, and experiential learning in various settings. Thus, the making of meaning is often interconnected with a sense of themselves as adults, as learners, and as social citizens.

Adult higher education recognizes that adults become more varied and differentiated as they advance through the life cycle (Cross, 1981). The variation includes significant elements, such as developmental stages (cognitive or moral, for example), knowledge and experience base, citizen identity and activity, and resources for learning beyond the campus. Consequently, many adult learner programs offer a more flexible and sometimes individualized approach to the curriculum. Increasingly, adult students assume a major role in tailoring areas of concentration, or in some cases whole programs, to address their knowledge and competence needs as workers, parents, and citizens. While faculty continue to play important roles as knowledge sources, they share this responsibility with various authorities outside the academy, as well as with the expertise of the adult learner.

Adult learning within literacy training and employee development in business and professional settings also illustrates the split between formal learning in an academic context and learning for direct, everyday performance in the adult world. Key differences exist between assessment for abstract knowledge and objective, noncontextual problem solving, and the real world of solving messy problems and creating knowledge in the complex contexts of adult lives. In these settings, to know and apply what is known is to be effective. Assessment of adult learners moves beyond the knowledge of abstract content to the world of situated cognition. Here the importance of context in establishing meaningful connections among knowledge, skills, and experience becomes one of the cornerstones for the creation and implementation of assessment approaches.

Principles for Adult-Oriented Learning Assessment

We propose five key principles that can guide adult-oriented assessment practices:

1. Learning is derived from multiple sources.
2. Learning engages the whole person and contributes to that person's development.
3. Learning and the capacity for self-direction are promoted by feedback.
4. Learning occurs in context; its significance relates in part to its impact on those contexts.
5. Learning from experiences is a unique meaning-making event that creates diversity among adult learners.

Table 1.1 lists five commonly held premises about adult learning from which these principles are derived (Chickering and Assoc., 1981; Dewey, 1938; Knowles, 1980; Kolb, 1984; Merriam and Caffarella, 1991; Mezirow, 1991; Schön, 1983). The principles can provide a framework for shaping adult-oriented assessment systems and strategies, for guiding authentic, relevant, and effective assessment of adult learning efforts. They can buttress good assessment practices in higher educational institutions, community education programs, and work and professional development efforts. The table might be read as making singular correspondences between the premises and the principles; however, this is not the case either in theory or in practice. Rather, in any given situation the premises and principles form an interactive and often synergistic matrix.

Table 1.1. Premises of Adult Learning and Interrelated Principles of Adult-Oriented Assessment Practice

Key Premises of Adult Learning	Key Principles of Adult-Oriented Assessment Practice
Learning is derived from multiple sources.	Recognizes multiple sources of knowing, that is, learning that occurs from interaction with a wide variety of informal and formal knowledge sources.
Learning engages the whole person and contributes to that person's development.	Recognizes and reinforces the cognitive, conative, and affective domains of learning.
Learning and the capacity for self-direction are promoted by feedback.	Focuses on adults' active involvement in learning and assessment processes, including active engagement in self-assessment.
Learning occurs in context; its significance relates in part to its impact on those contexts.	Embraces adult learners' involvement in and impact on the broader world of work, family, and community.
Learning from experiences is a unique meaning-making event that creates diversity among adult learners.	Accommodates adult learners' increasing differentiation from one another given varied life experiences and education.

PRINCIPLE 1. *Adult-oriented assessment recognizes multiple sources of knowing, that is, learning that occurs from interaction with a wide variety of informal and formal knowledge sources.*

Perhaps the most distinctive characteristic of adult learners is that they bring rich and varied experiences to the learning setting. They learn by integrating formal academic knowledge with their personal experience in their life context. Information they encounter in a classroom context is filtered through reflections on their experiences and understandings—past and present—and on their current actions. Those individuals who have rich, personal, and uniquely structured knowledge from the world of practice bring this knowledge and understanding into the classroom. They may actively judge the relevance of instructional content in terms of personal learning, they may consider alternative understandings, and they may explore broad philosophical and conceptual understandings in relation to the concrete phenomena of their daily lives. There are also those adults learners who selectively learn, apply, synthesize, and critically reflect on new and old sources of knowledge from the world of their everyday life and work, and the world of formal knowledge (Kasworm, 1997).

As suggested by Kolb (1984), learning for adults becomes relearning. Old knowledge can become transformed knowledge. Recent research on situated cognition suggests that learning is not confined to formal learning environments nor gained only through the cerebral process of reading and speaking.

For example, effective learning can also occur through modeling expert performance roles in various settings (Lave and Wenger, 1991). Another view holds that learning is socially constructed and its meaning is continuously renegotiated. Thus adult assessment must not focus exclusively on academic knowledge structures; rather, it should focus as well on the social learning of the adult world and the relationships among multiple sources of knowledge that create meaningful learning.

Illustrations of Practice. Many adult programs have drawn on the Kolb (1984) experiential learning model and related situated cognition principles as conceptual frameworks for outcomes assessment. At the individual level, an important model of adult experiential learning is reflected in the abilities-based curriculum of Alverno College, which serves women of all ages. Alverno College faculty purposefully teach students to develop abilities that facilitate the "doing" of what they know through performance and action. The faculty believes that it is essential to teach students how to transfer abilities to new situations. One aspect of Alverno's multidimensional assessment program focuses on this set of desired outcomes (Deutsch, Kramp, and Roth, 1990).

An example of applying new learning to improve performance is reflected in a continuing education certification program for practicing veterinarians at Pennsylvania State University. The program's goals were to help veterinarians incorporate new knowledge and skills into their practices and to increase collaboration among veterinarians, dairy farmers, and continuing educators in order to enhance dairy production and herd management. Using industry-standard performance indicators, participants were assessed for baseline data during an early part of the program, and these assessments were repeated periodically throughout. According to the evaluation report, participating veterinarians developed closer working relationships with their clients and "added new services and implemented new management strategies on their clients' farms" (Moore, Sischo, and Hutchinson, 1996, p. 1087).

PRINCIPLE 2. Adult-oriented assessment recognizes and reinforces the cognitive, conative, and affective domains of learning.

Adult educators, as well as leading learning theorists, share the belief that significant adult learning experiences are cognitive and affective (that is, they influence attitudes and values) as well as conative. This belief is directly connected to the premise underlying the first principle—that learning is derived from multiple sources—and extends that principle to bringing assessment into the realm of how adults transform knowledge once they grasp it. Some adult programs also emphasize the ability to act on what one knows and can do, that is, the performance dimension of learning (Loacker and Mentkowski, 1993). Influenced by Bloom's (1954) taxonomy of educational objectives and by the praxis of knowing and doing, or reflective practice, as framed by Schön (1983), many adult programs explore ways to define student learning outcomes across these three domains.

Illustrations of Practice. The University of Phoenix, which serves the adult working professional, pays particular attention to the affective and conative sides of learning. Its mission reflects "adult-centered educational programs in which the learner is expected to apply new knowledge to the workplace, and to evaluate its effectiveness" (University of Phoenix, 1992, p. 7). Pivotal to these concerns is adult-centered affective learning, including the conative dimension. The university developed and recently validated the Affective Impact Inventory to measure personal and professional values, attitudes, and self-reported behaviors. Among the areas examined are commitment to teamwork and cooperation, effective oral and written communications, self-confidence and a sense of competence, and critical thinking and evaluation skills (1992, pp. xii–xiii). In the cognitive area, the university provides cognitive assessment feedback to students at the point of entry and again near graduation. The initial report, sent directly to the student, profiles academic strengths and weaknesses and offers suggestions for applying this self-knowledge to the student's beginning studies. A similar assessment is administered when students near graduation in order to clarify where they place in relation to their peers, how much they achieved in relation to their prematriculation capabilities, and where they now stand within their discipline and degree program.

In the College of Lifelong Learning in New Hampshire, faculty have experimented with learning outcomes measurement that focuses on the application of what has been learned in college courses. They have adopted the Alverno College model of performance-based assessment to evaluate the learning of adult students. Within this framework, faculty and students examine how explicit criteria, faculty and peer feedback, and student self-assessment influence learning and performance.

Ameritech's approach is also an example of iterative assessment and feedback to promote ongoing development of designated competencies. A leadership development program for frontline managers at this company is designed to help managers develop core competencies (such as performance management and planning) as measured against company benchmarks (C. Wagner, Ameritech Corporation, Chicago, Ill., personal communication with author, May 1997). Each manager is assessed on these competencies prior to the start of a five-day program, using a 360-degree approach that solicits views from the person's supervisor, peers, and subordinates, and from the manager herself through self-assessment. At the conclusion of the instructional program, each manager is assessed again, using the same 360-approach, and the results are used to develop an individualized development plan targeting areas for further improvement and the strategies best suited to that individual. For at least a six-month period, each manager consults every thirty days with her or his instructor and supervisor to get feedback on progress and obtain additional support as needed.

The National External Diploma Program, offered through the American Council on Education, "is a high school diploma program for mature adults who acquired their academic skill through life and work experiences and can demonstrate that competence in an applied performance assessment process" (American Council on Education, 1997). The program measures specific skills needed by a competent adult functioning in the modern world, such as oral and written communication skills; sensitivities to cultural diversity and the need for teamwork; the setting of career goals; the ability to manipulate, analyze, synthesize, and apply data in context; and the ability to learn how to learn. Adults demonstrate these skills and awarenesses in practical ways (such as by interpreting maps, solving life-related math problems, and writing opinion pieces for the newspaper) that foster additional learning in the process.

Similarly, in the undergraduate program of the School for New Learning at DePaul University, adult learners acquire and demonstrate competence in terms of what they value, what they know, and what they can do. The structure for assessment is provided by a competence framework consisting of fifty items distributed across five domains, including lifelong learning, world of work (focus area), and three liberal arts-related areas. Assessment strategies serve to elevate students' awareness of the competencies they already possess in the context of their goals. Periodic assessment throughout the program then serves to monitor progress and to guide revisions to students' learning plans. As students approach graduation, assessment takes on a more summative focus, helping students to examine what they have accomplished and to look beyond the formalities of the undergraduate degree per se. Assessment then serves multiple functions: to affirm learning, to align cognitive efforts with values and goals, and to identify additional learning needs.

PRINCIPLE 3. *Adult-oriented assessment focuses on adults' active involvement in learning and assessment processes, including active engagement in self-assessment.*

One of the characteristics of adult development, and an outcome of the second premise of adult learning, is the emergence and evolution of the "self" and the movement of adults toward autonomy, self-agency, and the construction of knowledge. Two related aspects of learning assessment for adults in degree programs are that students should develop awareness of their own independence to act as educated individuals, and that the academic community should foster students' increased independence and self-directedness.

Illustrations of Practice. An interesting example comes from the University of Southern California regarding physician continuing education. This project identified the learning needs of physicians and used assessment data to engage them in modifying and improving their practice routines (Manning, Lee, Denson, and Gilman, 1980; Manning and others, 1986). As a backdrop to identifying learning needs, each of the participating physicians submitted an initial set of two hundred prescriptions that were analyzed by a faculty committee to identify problems in prescribing. Based on this analysis, 12.8 problems (such as improper dosage, high potential for adverse reactions, and equally effective drug available at less cost) were identified per one hundred prescriptions. Each of the participating physicians then received an instructional packet that included a statement of the prescribing problems, brief advice prepared by a committee member, copies of the original prescriptions, and copies of pertinent journal articles regarding current best practice.

This comprehensive feedback encouraged the physicians to make ongoing improvements in their current practice and to assess these improvements. One follow-up assessment showed that in relation to their self-reported intent to change, physicians made 30 percent of the recommended changes in prescribing; another assessment measure indicated that 50 percent of the physicians demonstrated change in prescribing. In this assessment-driven learning activity, the connection among self-directed learning, assessment, and practice was clearly demonstrated.

Some adult-oriented programs treat self-assessment as a pivotal component of their overall assessment process. In the Master of Arts for Integrated Professional Studies program of the School for New Learning at DePaul University, self-assessment is built into the core liberal learning curriculum. Over a two-year period, students periodically assess their development of specific liberal learning skills, how these are being applied in their work lives, and with what impact. They communicate their self-assessments in written essay form and during a group assessment session with their faculty mentor. Students report that intentional engagement in self-assessment practices throughout the program increases their self-directed learning capabilities, enhances their internal locus of control, improves their interpersonal skills, and increases their sense of personal and professional competence, particularly as they function in the workplace (Marienau, 1992, in progress).

PRINCIPLE 4. Adult-oriented assessment embraces adult learners' involvement in and impact on the broader world of work, family, and community.

Assessment should help validate what adult learners apply in the various contexts of their lives. This extends the first principle—adults learn from multiple sources—to the various communities of practice and application in which adults participate, elevating the impact that learning has on the circles of possible influence that surround adults. From an institutional or organizational point of view, educational or training programs should look to strategies and methods that incorporate feedback from these various communities in generating outcomes assessment data. These strategies would capture the impact of learning outcomes through such methods as surveys of employers, focus groups with family members, and surveys of adult learners as alumni or participants in programs.

Illustrations of Practice. A unique outcome assessment area at Thomas A. Edison State College is called System Building. After surveying more than two hundred educational institutions and government, military, corporate, and community entities that are part of their organizational network, administrators used the feedback to strengthen those relationships deemed vital to the direct instruction and support of adult learners. Results from this assessment help the college identify ways to assist organizations, increase their services to learners, and enhance opportunities for access to higher education (Thomas A. Edison State College, 1988). Follow-up studies of graduates provide evidence that alumni of Thomas Edison have found value and relevance in their educational experiences and accomplishments (Streckewald, 1992). Three of every five respondents reported that their job performance had improved as a result of the degree. Nearly half of the respondents reported receiving raises or promotions because of a college degree. Both of these findings suggest that adults' learning in college can have an impact within their communities of practice.

The University of Phoenix (1992) directs part of its assessment efforts toward determining the impact of both student and program on the employing organization. They obtain feedback from employers through focus groups, telephone surveys, and mailed surveys. These assessments focus on organizational and economic impact, such as students' capstone research projects that have been implemented within their current work environments or that have stimulated perceived increases in organizational productivity. The assessments also glean information regarding student growth in areas such as written and oral skills, team efforts, planning skills, and initiatives to assume greater responsibilities.

PRINCIPLE 5. *Adult-oriented assessment accommodates adults' increasing differentiation from one another given varied life experiences and education.*

The uniqueness of experience, the unpredictability of its interpretation, and the individuality of meaning-making lead to both a staggering diversity among adult learners and a challenge to practitioners of assessment. These elements underscore the principle that assessment should accommodate differences among adults. It also raises various questions that must be addressed before assessment activities can be employed at either the individual or collective level. For example, what characteristics best describe variation among adults? How might these characteristics be measured? If changes are demonstrated, which ones are most meaningful to the individual? To the organization? What validity do individual measures of learning hold? How might such outcomes information be used?

Illustrations of Practice. One pragmatic approach is to have adult learners participate, as Fox (1992) suggests, in the committees charged with shaping assessment goals and plans. In this setting, adult learners would have some voice in designing and modifying assessment instruments, in creating strategies for data collection, and in considering implications of the findings. Another pragmatic approach is represented by institutions (such as Thomas A. Edison State College and Phoenix University) that use focus groups with adult students to obtain their views on areas such as access, academic quality, services, and delivery systems, as well as the relevance of courses to adults' lives.

Beyond these practical ways to include adult learners' varying perspectives in the assessment effort, there still exists the challenge of how to think about and act on the phenomenon of great individual variation among adult learners. Drawing on their experience with student self-evaluations at Evergreen State College, Moore and Hunter (1993) offer a taxonomy to help address the individual-institution interaction as seen from differing viewpoints of assessment and research. "From a research perspective, the focus on the individual provides a potential source of important information on developmental patterns in learning: Who learns what? when? how? why?" (p. 68). From an assessment perspective, "the individual level is important because of the learning opportunity inherent in the self-evaluation and self-reflection process" (p. 69).

Testimony to this approach comes also from the Literacy South project, a two-year staff-development process with fifty-five adult literacy practitioners using portfolio assessment. Ninety-five percent of the teachers involved in this project reported that their practice had become more learner-centered and that portfolio assessment provided them with more information about their students' learning than other assessment methods. As suggested in the final report of this project, "a participatory approach to assessment or authentic assessment . . . allows for self-reporting in diverse ways which enable students to shine while using methods that are familiar to their cultures and experiences" (Schneider, Fingeret, and McGrail, 1997, p. 11).

The issue of normative standards versus individualized contexts is implicit in the statement just quoted. Capital University has come to know this issue intimately due to their long-term efforts to "home grow" instruments that are tailored to campus-specific questions about adult learning outcomes. An account of their experiences reveals some unplanned benefits (Ashbrook, Schalinske, and Patterson, 1995). For example, "individualized reports on academic proficiency and learning style were created from the data and sent to the students and their advisors. In a short period of time, these assessment results became an important component of academic advising, allowing advisors to better counsel students on effective adaptation to college" (p. 79). In addition, "a series of comparisons between profiles of traditional and adult learners heightened debate over pedagogical differences between the two programs, leading to a broader recognition of experiential learning and independent studies by traditional faculty, and a wider acceptance of non-traditional teaching methods throughout the campus" (p. 79).

Conclusion

The intent of this chapter has been to help stimulate dialogue within those environments where adult learners are learning and being assessed. The five key principles and related premises about adult learning that were presented can guide adult-oriented assessment. Quality outcomes assessment can contribute to improvements within educational programs of organizations, institutions of higher education, and various arenas of professional practice. Adult-oriented assessment suggests that affective outcomes, self-directed learning, and responsiveness to adult life circumstances are key areas to be considered beyond the traditional cognitive pretest and posttest efforts of many programs. Assessment that is centered in adult learning will consider the community of social practice, critical reflections on applications of knowledge, and knowledge that contributes to meaning-making in the context of various adult roles.

References

American Council on Education. *The National External Diploma Program, Public Information Packet.* Washington, D.C.: American Council on Education, 1997.

Ashbrook, R., Schalinske, R., and Patterson, R. "Choice and Consequence in the Assessment of Adult Learning Outcomes." *Proceedings for the Fifteenth Annual Alliance/American Council on Education Conference,* Columbus, Ohio, Oct. 1995.

Banta, T. *Are We Making a Difference?* San Francisco: Jossey-Bass, 1993.

Bloom, B. S. (ed.). *Taxonomy of Educational Objectives. Book 1: Cognitive Domain.* New York: Longman, 1954.

Chickering, A., and Associates. *The Modern American College.* San Francisco: Jossey-Bass, 1981.

Choi, J., and Hannafin, M. "Situated Cognition and Learning Environments: Roles, Structures, and Implications for Design." *Educational Technology: Research and Design,* 1995, 43 (2), 53–69.

Cross, K. P. *Adults as Learners.* San Francisco: Jossey-Bass, 1981.

Deutsch, B., Kramp, M. K., and Roth, J. L. "Alverno College." In A. Mandell and E. Michelson (eds.), *Portfolio Development and Adult Learning: Purposes and Strategies.* Chicago: Center for Adult and Experiential Learning, 1990.

Dewey, J. *Experience and Education.* London: Crollier-Macmillan, 1938.

Fox, P. "Involving Adult Students in Assessment." *Adult Assessment Forum,* 1992, 2 (1), 11.

Kasworm, C. "Adult Meaning-Making in the Undergraduate Collegiate Classroom." Paper presented at the American Educational Research Association, Chicago, Ill., Mar., 1997.

Knowles, M. *The Modern Practice of Adult Education: From Pedagogy to Andragogy.* (2nd ed.) New York: Cambridge Books, 1980.

Kolb, D. *Experiential Learning: Experience as the Source of Learning and Development.* Englewood Cliffs, N.J.: Prentice Hall, 1984.

Lave, J., and Wenger, E. *Situated Learning: Legitimate Peripheral Participation.* Cambridge: Cambridge University Press, 1991.

Loacker, G., and Mentkowski, M. "Creating a Culture Where Assessment Improves Learning." In T. Banta (ed.), *Are We Making a Difference?* San Francisco: Jossey-Bass, 1993.

Manning, P., Lee, P., Clintworth, W., Denson, T., Oppenheimer, P., and Gilman, N. "Changing Prescribing Practices Through Individual Continuing Education." *Journal of the American Medical Association,* 1986, 256 (2), 230–233.

Manning, P., Lee, P., Denson, T., and Gilman, N. "Determining Educational Needs in the Physician's Office." *Journal of the American Medical Association,* 1980, 244 (10), 112–114.

Marienau, C. "Enhancing Workplace Learning Through Self-Assessment in Graduate Education." Interim report for the National Center on Adult Learning, Empire State College, 1992.

Marienau, C. "Self-Assessment at Work: An Agent of Continuous Learning, Competent Performance, and Personal Development." Manuscript in progress.

Merriam, S., and Caffarella, R. *Learning in Adulthood: A Comprehensive Guide.* San Francisco: Jossey Bass, 1991.

Mezirow, J. *Transformative Dimensions of Adult Learning.* San Francisco: Jossey Bass, 1991.

Moore, W., and Hunter, S. "Beyond 'Mildly Interesting Facts': Student Self-Evaluations and Outcomes Assessment." In J. MacGregor (ed.), *Student Self-Evaluation: Fostering Reflective*

Learning. New Directions for Teaching and Learning, no. 56. San Francisco: Jossey-Bass, 1993.

Moore, D., Sischo, W., and Hutchinson, L. "Effect of Participation of Veterinarians in a Dairy Production Medicine Continuing Education Course on Management Practices and Performance of Client Herds." *Journal of American Veterinary Medical Association,* 1996, *209* (6), 1087–1089.

Schneider, M., Fingeret, H., and McGrail, L. *Phenomenal Changes: Stories of Participants in the Portfolio Project.* Raleigh, N.C.: Literacy South, 1997.

Schön, D. A. *The Reflective Practitioner: How Professionals Think in Action.* New York: Basic Books, 1983.

Spille, H. "Response to the Recommendations of the Goal 5 Task Force Report on Collegiate Assessment." *The Center Update* (The Center for Adult Learning and Educational Credentials, American Council on Education), 1993, *80,* 3–5.

Streckewald, T. C. *The Use of Survey Research in an Outcomes Assessment Program.* Trenton, N.J.: Thomas A. Edison State College, May 1992.

Thomas A. Edison State College. *Outcomes Assessment at Thomas A. Edison State College: First Annual Report, July 1987–June 1988.* Trenton, N.J.: Thomas A. Edison State College, September 1988.

University of Phoenix. "Assessing Development of Professional Values in the Working Adult College Student." Report IR–92.1. Phoenix, Ariz.: University of Phoenix, Department of Institutional Research, June 1992.

Young, M. F. "Instructional Design for Situated Learning." *Educational Technology Research and Development,* 1993, *41* (1), 43–58.

CAROL E. KASWORM *is professor of adult education and associate dean for research and technology at the University of Tennessee, Knoxville.*

CATHERINE A. MARIENAU *is associate professor in the School for New Learning at DePaul University, Chicago.*

*Based on a belief that critical thinking is a socially constructed process
and contextual in nature, the author challenges the use of standardized
assessments and instead offers locally grounded strategies.*

Assessing Critical Thinking

Stephen D. Brookfield

Critical thinking occupies a special place in the hearts of adult educators, particularly because of its connections to the democratic tradition that informs the
field. At the heart of a strong, participatory democracy is citizens' capacity to
question the actions, justifications, and decisions of political leaders, and the
capacity to imagine alternatives that are more fair and compassionate than current structures and moralities. Such capacities develop as we learn to think
critically. Encouraging critical thinking in adults is therefore integral to the
democratic project. It is also true that critical thinking seems to hold the
promise of constituting a universal theory of adult learning and, by implication, a template for adult education practice. If critical thinking is a uniquely
adult learning process, then fostering critical thinking becomes, by implication, a uniquely adult educational process. Critical thinking can be analyzed
in terms of both process and purpose, although these two elements are
inevitably intertwined.

The Process of Critical Thinking

As a process, critical thinking involves adults in recognizing and researching
the assumptions that undergird their thoughts and actions (Brookfield, 1987).
Assumptions are the taken-for-granted beliefs about the world and our place
within it that seem so obvious to us that they do not seem to need to be stated
explicitly. Assumptions give meaning and purpose to who we are and what we
do. In many ways we are our assumptions. So much of what we think, say, and
do is based on assumptions about how the world should work and about what
counts as appropriate, moral action. Yet frequently these assumptions are not
recognized for the provisional understandings they really are. Ideas and actions
that we regard as commonsense conventional wisdoms are often based on

uncritically accepted assumptions. Some person, institution, or authority that we either trust or fear has told us that this is the way things are and we have accepted their judgment unquestioningly. When we think critically, we start to research these assumptions for the evidence and experiences that inform them.

The purpose of critical thinking tends to be to scrutinize two particular and interrelated sets of assumptions. First, there are assumptions that frame how we view power relationships in our lives. Critical thinking entails adults understanding that the flow of power is a permanent presence in our lives. In our personal relationships, work activities, and political involvements, power relations are omnipresent, though often submerged. Uncovering and questioning these power relations so that we might redirect the flow of power in a circular or democratic manner is an important part of critical thinking.

Second, there are hegemonic assumptions that need to be uncovered. Hegemonic assumptions are those that we embrace eagerly because we think they are in our own best interests. Yet perversely these assumptions actually work against us in the long term and serve the purposes of those who do not have our best interests at heart. The term *hegemony* applies to the process whereby ideas, structures, and actions come to be seen by the majority of people as wholly natural, preordained, and working for their own good when in fact these ideas, structures, and actions are constructed and transmitted by powerful minority interests to protect the status quo that serves these interests so well. The subtle cruelty of hegemony is that over time it becomes deeply embedded, part of the cultural air we breathe. One cannot peel back the layers of oppression and identify a group or groups of people as the instigators of a conscious conspiracy to keep people silent and disenfranchised. Instead, the ideas and practices of hegemony become part and parcel of everyday life—the stock opinions, conventional wisdoms, or commonsense ways of seeing and ordering the world that people take for granted.

The Debate

One of the most intense debates about critical thinking concerns its assessment. How do we judge whether or not our efforts as adult educators are having any effect? How do we know that people are thinking, much less acting, critically? To be sure, several standardized tests are available that purport to measure students' ability to reason in a critical manner (Carpenter and Doig, 1988). Such tests tend to treat critical thinking as if it were a generic intellectual capacity that manifests itself in broadly similar ways across disciplines (Norris and Ennis, 1989). Others have argued that critical thinking needs to be assessed in the multiple contexts in which it occurs (Cromwell, 1992). The debate regarding the generalizability or specificity of critical thinking is foundational and unresolved (McPeck, 1990; Norris, 1992).

My own view of critical thinking is that it is irrevocably context bound. The same person can be highly critical in one situation, or with regard to one set of ideas, but completely closed to reappraising another situation or idea critically.

I also believe that learning to think critically is an irreducibly social process. It happens best when we enlist the help of other people to see our ideas and actions in new ways. Very few of us can get very far probing our assumptions on our own. No matter how much we may think we have an accurate sense of ourselves, we are stymied by the fact that we are using our own interpretive filters to become aware of our own interpretive filters! This is the pedagogical equivalent of a dog trying to catch its tail. A self-confirming cycle often develops whereby our uncritically accepted assumptions shape actions that then serve only to confirm the truth of those assumptions. We find it very difficult to stand outside ourselves and see how some of our most deeply held values and beliefs lead us into distorted and constrained ways of being. To become critically reflective, we need to find some lenses that reflect back to us a stark and differently highlighted picture of who we are and what we do. Our most influential assumptions are too close to us to be seen clearly by an act of self-will.

If critical thinking is conceived as an irreducibly social process, then our peers (and teachers) become important critical mirrors. When our peers listen to our stories and then reflect back to us what they see and hear in those stories, we are often presented with a version of ourselves and our actions that comes as a surprise. Hearing the perceptions of our peers helps us to gain a clearer perspective on the dimensions of our thoughts and actions that need closer critical scrutiny. Talking to others helps us to become aware of how much we take for granted about our own ideas and actions. It also alerts us to our judgmental ways of seeing. Sometimes it confirms the correctness of instincts that we felt privately but doubted because we thought they contradicted conventional wisdom.

Accurate assessment springs from an informed understanding of the phenomenon being studied, and the assessment of critical thinking is no exception. If critical thinking is context and person specific, if its manifestation is irrevocably embedded in its cultural surroundings, then an intelligent approach to assessment requires that it be grounded in local conditions. Assessing critical thinking really has to be locally crafted by those integrally involved with the process. It makes no sense to import formal tests devised by those outside the immediate context in which the critical thinking to be assessed is taking place.

In addition, if critical thinking is necessarily a social process, then it follows that its assessment should also be a social process involving a multiplicity of experiences, contributions, and perceptions.

This chapter outlines a number of examples of locally crafted, cooperative approaches to assessing critical thinking. These approaches are premised on three assumptions, which themselves should be subject to constant critical scrutiny:

1. *Critical thinking can be assessed only in specific contexts.* This means that studying the dimension of action—what students do as well as what they say—is crucial.

2. *Critical thinking can often be best assessed by one's peers, who function as critical mirrors.* Not only the instructor but also other learners can provide valuable assessment of one's developing capacity to question hegemonic assumptions and imagine democratic alternatives.
3. *Assessment of critical thinking should allow learners to document, demonstrate, and justify their own engagement in critical thinking.* In viewing learning from the outside, instructors may miss entirely the critical dimensions of students' thought and practice.

Please remember that the approaches to developing critical thinking outlined in this chapter are not a template. For me to propose a set of replicable, transferable, standardized methods for assessing critical thinking would be to undercut my own argument that it is a local, socially constructed process. If you choose to adapt any of my suggestions, do so with a great deal of reflective skepticism. These approaches are described here in the hope that they may get you started on your own efforts at crafting some locally grounded assessment procedures.

A Pretest and Posttest Approach: The Scenario Analysis Technique

One of the problems with developing local assessment approaches is that licensing bodies and accrediting agencies demand standardized mechanisms for documenting the development of critical thinking in students over time. Telling these organizations that no universal measures of critical thinking are appropriate is politically dangerous. It may mean that your program's reputation or credibility will be tarnished, or even that certification will be withdrawn. One way through this dilemma is to develop what looks like a series of pretest and posttest measures that are actually locally sculpted and responsive to context. An example of this is scenario analysis.

Analyzing familiar ideas and actions critically is an unfamiliar and intimidating process for most people. Adults need to begin a critical thinking program by learning the protocols and habits of critical thinking in relatively nonthreatening ways. As they gain confidence in their critical faculties by learning the habit of assumption hunting, they can be moved into the more threatening activity of applying critical thinking to their own lives, ideas, and actions.

The scenario analysis technique is a useful way to begin a critical thinking program. In scenario analysis students are presented with a hypothetical scenario in which a central character is making some kind of decision or initiating some kind of action. Learners are asked to put themselves in the place of the protagonist in the scenario and to write down the assumptions under which they think this person is acting. They are then asked to take each of the assumptions they think the protagonist holds and say how the protagonist might check them for accuracy and validity. Finally, they are asked to make an alternative interpretation of the scenario that the protagonist would disagree with if she or he were confronted by it.

The following scenario analysis exercise, called "Going Back," is an example of how the technique works:

Karen, a wife and mother of two young children in her thirties, has decided to go back to work. She has watched as her husband Jack, a busy professor, has taken on more and more work outside of his college to help provide his family with a decent quality of life in the city. She sees how tired he is and hears his complaints of how he never has enough time with his family, how he is being pulled in so many different directions, and how he wishes things would just slow down.

To ease the situation, Karen accepts a full-time job with a company in the suburbs. She will put the children into day care and commute back and forth each day to her work. She reckons that with the money her job brings into the home Jack will be able to give up many of his commitments outside of the college. This will give him more time with his family and reduce the pressures and tensions he feels. Overall, the family will be happier; their economic situation will be the same but the burden of producing income will be shared more fairly and Jack will be able to spend more time at home.

1. What assumptions—explicit and implicit—do you think Karen is operating under in this situation? List as many as you can.
2. Of the assumptions you have listed, which ones could Karen check by simple research and inquiry? How could she do this?
3. Give an alternate interpretation of this scenario—a version of what's happening that is consistent with the events described but that you think Karen would disagree with.

Here is one reading of the assumptions underlying Karen's actions that a group of adult students uncovered in this scenario:

1. Jack has been honest in what he is telling Karen. He wants more time with his family and wants to slow down his life.
2. It is up to Karen to fix the problem.
3. Fairness is an objective concept on which couples can agree.
4. The family's problems are financially based.
5. Families are happier when the burden of producing income is shared.
6. Women should stay at home with young children.
7. Jack will feel less pressure if Karen works.
8. Karen's working will reduce Jack's tension, the tension between Karen and Jack, and the tension between Jack and the rest of the family.
9. Spending more time with the family will reduce the pressure Jack feels.

Here is how the group split these assumptions into assumptions of power and assumptions of hegemony:

Assumptions of Power

1. The problem is Karen's to solve (by getting a job). Her taking a job will reduce familial tension, decrease the pressure Jack feels, and therefore help the situation.
2. It's Karen's responsibility to find and fund day care and to find good paying work.

Assumptions of Hegemony

1. Money is the cause of the family's stress.
2. Money is the solution to the family's problems.
3. The only way for this situation to be resolved is for Karen to find a job.
4. Karen's job will provide more money, and therefore more family happiness.

The assumptions in the second cluster are hegemonic because they reinforce the cultural ideal that money brings happiness. They meet the three conditions of a hegemonic assumption: it is widely accepted as being common sense; it ends up harming us and working against our physical, psychological, and political health; and it serves the interests of another group (the producers of goods who benefit from our consuming their goods).

The scenario analysis exercise can be adapted to a pretest-posttest assessment format by posing several general scenarios to students at the start of an educational program. Doing this introduces them to the habit of identifying assumptions, searching for ways to check them out, and generating multiple perspectives. Then, as students become familiar with the process, they can be asked to analyze scenarios that are specific to an activity or knowledge area of concern.

Using the three questions posed in the Going Back scenario for each subsequent scenario allows for a degree of comparison. Over time you can see whether learners are able to identify more assumptions, propose more diverse methods to research them, and generate increasingly greater numbers of alternative readings. You can also design the scenarios to involve greater degrees of complexity, perhaps by introducing multiple actors or by adding intractable ethical issues. If people are able to identify several assumptions, propose several ways to check them out, and generate several alternative interpretations or perspectives, then you can reasonably argue that their capacity to think critically is growing.

The problem with this approach is that it is not a valid measure. It does not address the quality of the analysis. Are the assumptions, ways of checking, and alternative interpretations plausible in the scenario? And who decides whether they are plausible—the designers of the scenario? the readers? knowledgeable outside parties? or all of these? My own preference is for decisions about the plausibility of responses to become an item for critical conversation.

An Experiential Approach: The Critical Practice Audit

Students who are learning to think critically about some aspect of their work may find the critical practice audit to be useful. The audit uses a critical incident approach to help workers focus on the extent to which critical analysis is evident in their practice. The term *critical practice* refers to any work people do that involves analyzing situations, reflecting on past experience, making judgments and decisions, and taking actions without the benefit of a standard protocol or uniform response that takes care of each and every problem they encounter. The audit has been used mostly with teachers and nurses.

Following are the instructions for conducting a critical practice audit:

• Please complete this audit on a weekly basis. Its purpose is to help you understand more about your own practice—in particular, to help you understand the assumptions that undergird how you analyze situations, make decisions, and take actions.

• Please think back over the past seven days. As you review your clinical practice, think about the critical incidents that have happened during that time. A critical incident is an event that can be called to mind easily and quickly because it is remembered vividly. We usually consider critical events to be significant because they are unexpected—they take us by surprise. Sometimes they are wonderful highs, sometimes they are demoralizing lows. Often they are a mix of both.

• Choose the most memorable two or three critical incidents in your clinical practice over the last seven days. For each incident, do the following:

1. Write a brief description of the incident, including details of what happened, who was involved, where and when it took place, and what made the incident critical for you.
2. List the assumptions you have as a clinical practitioner that were confirmed by this incident. What was it about what happened that led you to think that the assumptions you uncovered were accurate and valid?
3. List the assumptions you have as a clinical practitioner that were challenged by this incident. What was it about what happened that led you to think the assumptions you uncovered might be inaccurate or invalid?
4. How did you try to check the accuracy of your assumptions that were challenged? If you were not able to check them at the time, how could you check them in the future? What sources of evidence could you consult?
5. What different perspectives could be taken on the incident? As you think about it through the eyes of the other people involved, are there different ways the situation could be seen, or that your behavior could be interpreted?
6. In retrospect, are there different responses you might have made to the incident? If so, what would these responses be and why would you make them?

As learners respond to these questions on a weekly basis, they are documenting their growing capacity for, and struggles with developing, critical thinking. The critical practice audit is similar to the scenario analysis in that people are asked to focus on how their actions in specific circumstances reveal the assumptions they hold. The difference is that the actions and actors are real, not fictional.

A Behavioral Approach: Critical Debate

Another way to bring learners into the critical thinking process is to engage them in a critical debate, a theatrical device with an element of playful swagger built into it. As such, it draws in students who feel it will not involve their "real" selves in any serious consideration of new ideas. But as the process evolves, students find themselves deeply engaged in taking alternative perspectives on familiar ideas. The following instructions show how the process works:

- Find a contentious issue on which opinion is divided among participants. Frame the issue as a debate motion.
- Propose the motion to participants. By a show of hands ask people either to volunteer to work on a team that is preparing arguments to support the motion, or to volunteer to work on a team that is preparing arguments to oppose the motion.
- Announce that all those who volunteered for the supporting team will actually be on the opposing team, and vice versa.
- Conduct the debate. Each team chooses one person to present their arguments. After initial presentations the teams reconvene to draft rebuttal arguments and choose one person to present these.
- Debrief the debate. Discuss with participants their experience of this exercise. Focus on how it felt to argue against positions to which they were committed. What new ways of thinking about the issue were opened up? Did participants come to new understandings? Did they change their positions on the issue at all?
- Ask participants to write a follow-up reflection paper on the debate according to the following instructions:

  1. What assumptions about the issue were clarified or confirmed for you by the debate?
  2. Which of your assumptions were you surprised by during the debate? In other words, which assumptions that you did not know you held were you made aware of during or after the debate?
  3. How could you check out these new assumptions? What sources of evidence could you consult?
  4. What new perspectives on the issue suggested themselves to you?
  5. In what ways, if any, were your existing assumptions challenged or changed by the debate?

As learners debate, the instructor has the chance to assess their capacity to engage in perspective taking. Faculty and students together can discuss their ability to see things from a markedly different perspective. If a small group of students is asked to observe the debate rather than participate in it, they can report back to the group their assessment of how things went.

The five questions just outlined can form the basis of an assessment measure if answers are gathered together in a critical portfolio and read over time. These responses allow the instructor to assess the extent to which students are engaged in the three processes of critical thinking: identifying assumptions, researching them, and generating multiple perspectives.

A Conversational Approach: Storytellers and Detectives

One of the hardest processes of critical thinking for students to learn, and for teachers to assess, is the ability to give challenging but respectful critical commentary on another person's ideas or actions. Given that we live in a culture infused with the dynamics of power, and that we rarely (if ever) have the chance to participate in or witness egalitarian group talk, most people do not know how it happens or what it looks like.

Any effort to assess people's attempts to think critically must involve gaging their ability to talk critically, to engage in critical conversation. A critical conversation is a focused conversation in which someone is helped to come to an awareness of the assumptions under which she is operating, to investigate the extent to which these assumptions are well grounded in critically examined reality, to look at her ideas and actions from different viewpoints, and to think about the implications of the conversation for her future actions. As a first stage in learning critical conversation, students often find the following Storytellers and Detectives Conversational Protocol helpful:

- In this exercise people play one of three possible roles:

1. *The storyteller:* the person who is willing to make herself the focus of critical conversation by first describing some part of her experience
2. *The detectives:* others in the group whose purpose is to help the storyteller examine her experience so that she comes to a more fully informed understanding of the assumptions that inform her ideas and actions
3. *The umpire:* the group member who monitors the conversation with a view to pointing out when people are talking to each other in a judgmental way

All participants in the group play all three of these roles at different times. The idea is that the behaviors associated with each role gradually become habitual. Here is how the exercise works:

The Storyteller Tells the Tale. The conversation opens with the person who is the storyteller describing as concretely and specifically as possible an incident from her experience that for some reason is lodged in her memory. This incident may be one that is recalled because it was particularly fulfilling or because it was particularly frustrating. The storyteller describes the incident without any questions or interruptions. Her colleagues, who are in the role of detectives, listen with a purpose.

The detectives are trying to identify the explicit and implicit assumptions about the experience that they hear in the storyteller's tale. They are asked to imagine themselves inside the heads of the other characters in the story and to try to see the events through their eyes. If possible, the detectives make mental or written notes about plausible alternative interpretations of the story that fit the facts as they hear them but that might come as a surprise to the storyteller.

The Detectives Ask Questions About the Event. After the storyteller has finished speaking, the detectives break their silence and ask any questions they have about the events she has just described. The detectives search for any information that will help them uncover the assumptions they think the storyteller holds. They also look for details not provided in the first telling of the story that will help them to relive the events described through the eyes of the other participants involved, thereby helping them to understand these events from the different participants' perspectives. The one ground rule they must observe is to request information, not to give judgment. Their questions are asked only for the purpose of clarifying the details of what happened. They must refrain from giving their opinions or suggestions, no matter how helpful they feel these might be.

As the storyteller hears the detectives' questions, she tries to answer them as fully and honestly as possible. She also has the opportunity to ask the detectives why they asked the particular questions they put to her. The umpire points out to the detectives any judgmental questions they ask, particularly those in which they imply that they have seen a better way to respond to the situation than the way that has been described. Examples of such questions would be those that begin, "Did you really believe that. . . ?" "Didn't you think to. . . ?" or "Do you mean to tell us that. . . ?" The umpire brings the detectives' attention to the ways in which their tone of voice and body language, as well as their words, risk driving the storyteller into a defensive bunker.

The Detectives Report the Assumptions They Hear. When the incident has been fully described, and all the detectives' questions have been answered, the conversation moves to the assumption-hunting phase. Here the detectives tell the storyteller, on the basis of her story and her response to their questions, what assumptions they think she holds. This is done nonjudgmentally, as a reporting-back exercise. The detectives seek only to state clearly what they think the storyteller's assumptions are, not to judge whether they are right or wrong. They are asked to state these assumptions tentatively, descriptively, and nonjudgmentally, using phrases like "It seems as if. . .," "I wonder if one assumption you might be holding is that. . .," or "Is it possible that you assumed that. . . ?" The umpire intervenes when she thinks the detectives are reporting assumptions with a judgmental overlay.

The Detectives Give Alternative Interpretations. The detectives now give alternative versions of the events described, based on their attempts to relive the story through the eyes of the other participants. These alternative interpretations must be plausible in that they must be consistent with the facts as they have been described by the storyteller. The umpire points out those moments when psychoanalytic second-guessing is taking place, when the detectives start to preface their interpretations with remarks like "You know, what you were really doing. . ." or "What was really going on here. . . ." Again, the detectives are to give these interpretations as descriptions, not as judgments. They are describing how others involved in the events might have viewed them, not saying whether these perceptions are accurate.

After the detectives have described how the situation might look through the eyes of other participants, the storyteller is allowed to give any additional information that would cast doubt on these interpretations. She is also allowed to ask the detectives to elaborate on any confusing aspects of their interpretations. She is not expected to agree with the detectives.

The Participants Do an Experiential Audit. Finally, the storyteller and the detectives state what they have learned, what insights they have realized, and what their reflection means for their future actions. The umpire also gives a summary of the ability of participants to be respectful listeners and talkers.

It is in this final audit or debriefing phase that some useful assessment work can take place. Of course the umpire's report is crucial. As well as giving an assessment of the group's ability to converse critically, the umpire can write private notes to participants that draw attention to what they have done well or badly, or hold conversations with them about these matters, or both. Such written and spoken encounters can focus on the very specific words, phrases, conversational patterns, tonal qualities, and gestures that either helped others to face assumptions they would rather not acknowledge, or caused them to become so defensive that they shut out all alternative perspectives.

The participants in a critical conversation can also assess their developing willingness, or their lack of willingness, to engage in critical conversation. After the conversation they can write a self-assessment report in which they document the ways they tried, as detectives, to phrase questions, report assumptions, and suggest perspectives in a challenging but nonconfrontational manner. Because all participants sooner or later act as storytellers, they can also write an evaluation of their colleagues' ability to give critique. This serves two functions. First, these observations can be shared with the individual colleagues to help them improve their capacity for critique. Second, as the storytellers reflect on how it felt to hear certain kinds of questions or listen to people offering assumptions and perspectives, they can gauge their own reactions. They can then use these reactions as stimuli to examine their own behaviors as givers of critique. For example, if certain ways of asking questions threaten or anger them, they can examine the extent to which they use the same forms of words when they ask questions of others.

There is also a role here for an experienced teacher to assess adults' developing capacities for critical conversation. If the group agrees to be videotaped, the teacher can use this tape as a record of what transpired. She can start out by showing examples of what she feels are helpful questions, and then she can check with the storyteller to see whether she agreed that they were helpful. The teacher can then provide examples of how certain ways of offering assumptions and suggesting new perspectives helped the storyteller to come to a clearer understanding of her own assumptions, and then again she should check with the storyteller to see whether the storyteller experienced these conversational interactions as helpful. The teacher's analysis will usually prompt a wider discussion among the group regarding helpful and unhelpful ways of giving critique.

Depending on the trust level, the teacher can then show examples of unhelpful, unnecessarily intimidating questions, disrespectful ways of offering assumptions, and threatening, insulting ways of suggesting different perspectives on the storyteller's actions. If possible, it is best to ask the participants themselves first to select what they feel were the worst examples of unhelpful, confusing, or insulting critique. If the teacher has been a participant in the conversation, she should go first in drawing attention to her own worst behaviors.

Conclusion: The Importance of Modeling in Assessing Critical Thinking

One of my strongest convictions about critical thinking is that students learn to think, write, and speak in critical and democratic ways by watching respected leaders in positions of power and authority model these processes in their own lives. So, one of the first things that teachers of critical thinking need to do is make sure that they model a public commitment to and engagement in critical thinking before they ask their own students to engage in critical thinking. This involves teachers' doing a continual public self-assessment of their facility for critical analysis.

There are various ways to do this. One is to talk out loud about their own estimation of how well they have participated in critical discourses while they are in the midst of it, drawing attention to a poorly phrased question or comment. They can also talk out loud about how their instincts and preferences shape a group's agenda, which is supposed to be collectively and democratically constructed. And they can assess the extent to which they conveniently omit ideas or evidence that contradicts their positions, or note the questions that went unanswered. I try to use a classroom critical incident questionnaire in every class, to clarify and challenge assumptions I have made about the course (Brookfield, 1995).

Teachers have to earn the right to ask students to take critical thinking seriously. Modeling critical thinking not only gives learners a model, scaffold, and point of access to the process, it also builds trust between learners and leaders. This insight applies just as much to assessment as to any other part of the educational process. Students will learn habits of critical self-assessment partly by watching how teachers engage in this process. So, part of being a good teacher of critical thinking is modeling a commitment to one's own engagement in critical self-assessment.

References

Brookfield, S. D. *Developing Critical Thinkers: Challenging Adults to Explore Alternative Ways of Thinking and Acting.* San Francisco: Jossey-Bass, 1987.

Brookfield, S. D. *Becoming a Critically Reflective Teacher.* San Francisco: Jossey-Bass, 1995.

Carpenter, C., and Doig, J. C. "Assessing Critical Thinking Across the Curriculum." In J. H. McMillan (ed.), *Assessing Students' Learning.* New Directions for Teaching and Learning, no. 34. San Francisco: Jossey-Bass, 1988.

Cromwell, L. S. "Assessing Critical Thinking." In C. A. Barnes (ed.), *Critical Thinking: Educational Imperative.* New Directions for Community Colleges, no. 77. San Francisco: Jossey-Bass, 1992.

McPeck, J. E. *Teaching Critical Thinking.* New York: Routledge, 1990.

Norris, S. P. (ed.), *The Generalizability of Critical Thinking: Multiple Perspectives on an Educational Ideal.* New York: Teachers College Press, 1992.

Norris, S. P., and Ennis, R. H. *Evaluating Critical Thinking.* Pacific Grove, Calif.: Midwest Publications, 1989.

STEPHEN D. BROOKFIELD holds the title of Distinguished Professor at the University of St. Thomas, St. Paul, Minnesota.

Noncollegiate sponsored programs of instruction bring to life the often-espoused belief that learning is acquired through experience and should be recognized appropriately.

The Assessment of Noncollegiate Sponsored Programs of Instruction

Richard J. Hamilton

Although most of this volume focuses on the assessment of individual learning, this chapter briefly changes the focus to the assessment of programs of instruction. The American Council on Education and the New York Board of Regents each sponsors a program that assesses instruction offered by noncollegiate organizations. Although many of the issues that arise in individual and programmatic assessment are similar, each type of assessment engenders distinct issues about quality and learning. Some of these distinctions are especially important for institutions of higher education. Therefore, in addition to setting a context and describing the process used to assess noncollegiate instruction, this chapter also discusses some of the distinct issues that pertain to the assessment of noncollegiate sponsored programs of instruction.

The Problem

Imagine that you are forty years old and have crafted a successful, twenty-year career with a manufacturing concern. You are proud that through hard work and intelligence you have progressed from apprentice technician to engineer. Now, because of a merger between your firm and a large international conglomerate, you are fearful that your position may be in jeopardy because you do not have a bachelor's degree. The new firm requires a minimum of a baccalaureate degree for engineers.

You immediately contact a local college that you have attended periodically and once again have them evaluate your credits. Now that the pressure is on, you are motivated to complete your bachelor of science degree in engineering technology. The evaluation you receive, which contains some creative

New Directions for Adult and Continuing Education, no. 75, Fall 1997 © Jossey-Bass Publishers interpretation of previous academic credits, puts you within a semester or two of acquiring the degree. But some of the remaining degree requirements appear silly given your experience as an engineer and you feel that the college is wasting your time and money. For example, to complete the bachelor of science degree in engineering technology you must earn three credits in technical writing, even though your success was built on your technical writing skills.

Some of your colleagues have received academic credit for the technical writing courses they completed within the company. You, too, have the certificates to prove that you attended the courses, and the products to demonstrate that you can generate successful reports, proposals, letters, and memoranda, but your college does not assess prior learning. You have investigated transferring to another college but you would lose too many credits because of their strict residency requirements. You feel trapped and frustrated.

This scenario repeats itself daily on college campuses. Adults returning to college face many barriers to success; they must resolve issues of time, distance, cost, disposition, and preparedness to do postsecondary work. But one of the most discouraging barriers for adults who are otherwise prepared for such study is the unwillingness or inability of institutions to recognize and accredit college-level learning acquired by these students through noncollegiate experiences. Adult students find it especially discouraging when colleges discount the sophisticated learning they have acquired through their employment. Little can stifle student motivation more than having to take a course in a subject already mastered simply because it is a curriculum requirement and the college has no mechanism for assessing prior learning or it has a policy prohibiting such assessments.

The Background

Over the centuries philosophers and educators alike have acknowledged the intimate relationship between experience and learning. From Aristotle through Aquinas, Locke and Kant to Dewey, there has been continuous philosophic agreement that in some way experience is indispensable to or synonymous with learning. This assumption about the value of experience and its relationship to learning became a central tenet of several recent movements in education, including prior learning assessment.

Prior learning assessment is a process of identifying, articulating, measuring, and accrediting learning that is acquired outside the traditional classroom and frequently prior to enrollment in college. The learning may be acquired through independent study or under the auspices of a corporation or other organization. The central tenet of prior learning assessment is that learning may occur in many different ways and places (Rose, 1989) and should be accredited.

The tumultuous and radical atmosphere on campus in the 1960s was geared primarily to demands by younger students for more academic freedom, but it also encouraged college educators to experiment and expand nontraditional programs for adults. The civil rights and women's movement further increased the stream of adults to campus and intensified the discussions on prior learning assessment. Many major reports of the period (Carnegie Commission on Higher Education, 1971a, 1971b, 1972; Commission on Non-Traditional Study, 1973) professed that learning could take place anywhere and that it should be credited when possible (Meyer, 1975). Gamson (1989) noted that some educators observed that many students could demonstrate that they already knew what the colleges wanted to teach them, and that recognizing this knowledge could shorten the time spent earning a degree. Educators therefore developed even broader programs to recognize this prior learning.

Willingham (1976) wrote that prior learning assessment was an important element in the reform of higher education that was "directed to the extension of educational opportunity, enhancement of lifelong learning, and the improvement of the relationship between education and work" (p. 224). Other educators viewed prior learning assessment as an opportunity to reform higher education by improving the educational experience and updating the objectives (p. 224). A number of innovative programs arose in response to this movement, including some forms of achievement testing, portfolio assessment, and the evaluation of noncollegiate sponsored instruction.

The Program

In response to the major studies on nontraditional education just noted, and to the success of the American Council on Education's (ACE) assessment of military training, the University of the State of New York initiated a pilot project in January 1974 to evaluate the instruction offered in noncollegiate settings. In August 1974, ACE joined the effort and both organizations agreed to operate under policies and procedures established jointly by ACE's Commission on Educational Credit and the New York Board of Regents. During the pilot stage, 102 courses sponsored by eight organizations in New York State were reviewed. The outcomes of the project included not only credit recommendations for courses found to be of college quality and level, but more importantly, the identification of procedures for a reliable system of evaluation. In September 1977, ACE withdrew from the joint program and began an independent program (American Council on Education, 1996b; Board of Regents of the University of the State of New York, 1996).

Currently there are two active programs that have similar missions and use essentially the same educational protocols. One is called the National Program on Noncollegiate Sponsored Instruction (PONSI) and is administered by the Board of Regents of the University of the State of New York. Since 1994, National PONSI has been run cooperatively by the Board of Regents of the University of the State of New York and the Board of Regents of California State University. The other program is administered by ACE and was referred to as ACE PONSI until recently, when ACE changed the name to CREDIT, which is short for An American Council on Education College Credit Recommendation Service.

The purpose of each program is to review formal instructional programs and courses sponsored by noncollegiate organizations and to make college-level credit recommendations. The programs are premised on the belief that it is sound educational practice to grant academic credit for learning acquired through high quality instructional programs conducted by noncollegiate organizations (American Council on Education, 1996b; Board of Regents of the University of the State of New York, 1996).

ACE PONSI (now CREDIT) reported early in 1997 that it had reviewed more than 6,800 courses from more than 250 institutions. Its credit recommendations are published annually in *The National Guide to Educational Credit for Training Programs* (American Council on Education, 1996b). National PONSI reported in 1996 that it too had served more than 250 organizations and reviewed more than 4,500 courses. Its biennial publication is now entitled *College Credit Recommendations: The Directory of the National Program on Noncollegiate Sponsored Instruction* (Board of Regents of the University of the State of New York, 1996). Although there are some subtle differences between the programs, each now evaluates noncollegiate instruction according to the protocols and criteria identified during the pilot project and refined through practice. For the purposes of the remainder of this chapter, these two programs are referred to jointly as PONSI.

All organizations seeking to have their programs assessed must submit an application that provides information on all aspects of program delivery, and undergo an in-depth evaluation that examines each course's content, the way the organization maintains records, and how each program is administered. Any noncollegiate organization offering instruction for its employees, members, or customers is eligible to submit courses for review. Appropriate institutions include businesses, labor unions, hospitals, government agencies, professional and voluntary organizations, and proprietary vocational schools. Organizations authorized to offer educational credits or academic degrees are not eligible for evaluation through PONSI. Thus, an institute offering noncredit courses and operating under the aegis of an accredited college is not eligible to have its courses reviewed. This policy eliminates the awkwardness that would arise from PONSI enabling such an institute to circumvent the traditional collegiate course approval process. Only courses or programs offered on a formal basis and with official approval of the organization are considered for review. Informal training, on-the-job training, and independent study are not eligible for review.

The criteria for the awarding of a PONSI credit recommendation involve the following:

- The organization must determine that its instruction is college level, that its courses are of appropriate duration, that it evaluates the participants' performance, and that the instructors are qualified to teach the course.
- Each course to be evaluated must have already been offered by the sponsoring organization within a set period prior to the evaluation, and complete documentation of programming must be provided.

- The organization must provide evidence that it maintains permanent, official records of students' participation and performance in each course. It must provide general information and data from four broad general categories: program administration, record keeping, instruction, and course development (American Council on Education, 1996a).
- The organization must provide comprehensive information on each course to be evaluated, including a course description, the course objectives, the outcomes that participants will have experienced upon completion of the course, and an outline of the instruction, the instructional methods used in the course, and the evaluation methods used to gauge students' success.
- The organization must describe the mechanisms used to determine whether participants have achieved the desired outcomes and the minimum standards for successful completion of the course. They must also describe what happens to participants who do not meet minimum standards.
- Applicants are asked to address other issues that are of importance to accredited institutions, including admissions requirements, class size, program enrollment, program need, competition from accredited institutions, prerequisites, attendance requirements, and the preparation time outside of the class that is expected of participants.

Once an application is completed, the materials are sent to PONSI for a determination that all minimum criteria for a review have been met. The information is then sent to the evaluation team members who have been recruited by PONSI. All reviewers are faculty from accredited colleges and universities or other acknowledged experts in their fields. The number of reviewers depends on the complexity of the subject offered in the course, but the smallest number used to review a single subject course is usually three faculty experts, who are assisted by a PONSI office representative.

Upon completion of the evaluation, the faculty make a credit recommendation, if warranted, which must include the number of credits recommended, the level of the credits, the effective dates of the evaluation, and a brief description of the course and the learning strategies used. If appropriate, an evaluation can be made retroactively; that is, if a program has remained substantially unchanged, the evaluation team may recommend that the credit recommendation be effective as of a date in the past. This date is generally no earlier than five years prior to the date of the evaluation. Each year the noncollegiate institutions are required to complete a report certifying that the course and the supporting administrative services remain substantially unchanged.

The cost of a program assessment is substantial. In addition to paying a base fee, which can be thousands of dollars, the organization pays an annual fee to PONSI to maintain the database and the credit registry service and to publish the relevant documents. Of course the fees vary with the number of programs or courses to be assessed. In addition to the set fees the organization pays at the beginning of the process, the organization is also responsible for all faculty travel expenses and for the modest stipend paid to the faculty assessors.

The Issues

In addition to the obvious differences of purpose between methods that assess individual learning (such as portfolio assessment) and PONSI, which assesses programs of learning, there are several other significant differences, including (1) the location of control of the learning strategies, (2) the control of the assessment process itself, and (3) the relationship of the assessment to the credit-granting authority.

In many models of portfolio assessment, the students control the structure, quality, and pace of the learning, but then also bear the responsibility of identifying, articulating, and demonstrating the learning that has been acquired. This process affords students many options. For example, they may choose to study independently or to contract with a vendor to provide instruction, or they may use a combination of many methods to acquire the needed learning. After completion of the learning process, students identify and articulate their significant learning and compile appropriate evidence to demonstrate competence to a qualified faculty assessor. This evidence is usually accompanied by a narrative that affords the learners the opportunity to examine their learning critically and thereby enhance its overall effect.

The assessor of the portfolio is essentially unconcerned about the learning methods that students used but very concerned about the nature and quality of the learning. After carefully reviewing students' evidence to verify the depth and breadth of their learning, the assessor reports the results through appropriate channels to the college. The college, through its faculty and institutional guidelines, maintains control of the assessment and the authority for awarding and recording credit recommendations. Weaknesses in this model include faculty apathy for participating in assessments, which results in unsubstantiated credit awards, lost opportunity for students to receive full recognition for their learning, or institutional policies and procedures that can be so complex and punitive that the assessment program is rendered ineffectual or unattainable.

In program assessment, the noncollegiate organization controls the structure, quality, and pace of the learning, bears the responsibility for identifying and articulating the learning objectives, and then is responsible for measuring the program's effectiveness. Students are limited to using the learning strategies offered in the program, which are probably more restricted than those in individually developed programs of assessment, such as portfolio assessment. The assessment of the organizational program, including its effectiveness, is controlled by consultants, usually college faculty experts, who are hired by PONSI. This puts both the control of the instruction and the assessment of the program outside the authority of the college and out of the control of its faculty. The college, however, retains the ultimate control—the right to establish policies and procedures for accepting (or not accepting) prior learning.

As in all assessment programs, there are real and perceived weaknesses in PONSI. Much of the technical criticism (that is, criticism of the structure and administration) of PONSI can be dismissed after careful analysis. For example, one could argue that the process of achieving consensus among faculty assessors on the credit value of a course serves to dilute the quality of the assessment and to inflate the amount of credits recommended, particularly because the assessors come from different institutions. This position is faulty for several reasons. By bringing in faculty from several different colleges, one obtains input from a cross section of accepted higher education practice within a discipline or for a specific course. This should be perceived as a strength because practice and modes of instruction vary among institutions and must be taken into account when assessing organizations' courses. Rather than being perceived as a dilution of the quality of the assessment of a course, using several experts should be seen as an appropriate mechanism for discussing the instructional methods, outcomes, and effectiveness of the course and as a means for obtaining an accurate and fair estimate of the academic value of the instruction. To limit an assessment to one segment of higher education (for example, to faculty from four-year schools) or to one evaluator would weaken the process.

Another possible complaint is the potential for a conflict of interest between the need for rigor in evaluating courses versus the need to please the sponsoring organization so that it will continue to participate in the PONSI process. For this reason PONSI assessments are similar to accreditation reviews. They are designed to assure quality and to win faculty approval. The assessments are concerned not only with the nature and quality of the learning but also with where and how this learning is acquired. Student records, institutional mission, finances, facilities, faculty qualifications, staff preparation, instructional methods, educational goals and objectives, and retention and graduation rates are all examined in detail by qualified faculty. The evaluation and reporting procedures are exacting, and appropriate for an academic evaluation, and the instructions to the faculty experts are precise. However, the ultimate responsibility for the determination of the credit worthiness of a course is clearly in the hands of the faculty experts. Faculty review the program and determine whether the instruction and outcomes are equivalent to those acquired in a similar course on campus. Furthermore, the PONSI guidelines for the faculty clearly delineate that they are compensated for their evaluation of the courses, not for the outcome of the assessment. That is, the assessors are not remunerated according to the number of credits they award. Thus any appearance of a conflict of interest is eliminated.

The protocols developed over the life of the PONSI programs have led to a technically solid assessment program that places learning first and acknowledges the complex nature of the interrelationship of knowledge, learning, and experience. Adult students access these credit recommendations and shorten the time necessary to earn a degree. The prototypical student described at the beginning of this chapter would certainly have benefitted from a PONSI review of corporate training.

To further strengthen the overall value of the assessment provided by the PONSI project, each of the PONSI organizations tracks the number of colleges that accept their recommendations. The current tally is more than 1,400. Many of the faculty conducting the evaluations are from institutions that accept the recommendations, and they are influential in setting policy on their campuses regarding the acceptance of nontraditional credit. In addition, National PONSI is now a partner with the California State University, and CREDIT is establishing a network of colleges to serve as state affiliates that conduct many of the assessments.

There is a philosophical issue that poses a question that is more serious than any technical limitations. Some critics of prior learning assessment believe that accepting credits from these assessments dilutes the value of a college degree and lessens the holistic nature of the collegiate experience. They argue correctly that college is more than the sum of several dozen courses, that instead it is a comprehensive learning experience that nurtures the growth of critical thinking and problem-solving skills, self-esteem, and self-confidence, and provides an environment that enables young adults to broaden their experience and mature with increasing responsibilities. This vision needs some revision when discussing adult collegians.

For the new adult majority on campus, a vision of college as a maturing and broadening experience in the sense that it is used for youth is inadequate. Most adults, as so eloquently described by Knowles (1970) and others, have already endured many broadening and maturing experiences, and many have also acquired some of the learning expected of college graduates. However, they have not acquired these experiences and the accompanying learning under collegiate tutelage, and this characteristic seems to lead to a hesitation in accepting and recognizing prior learning. Cremin (1989, p. 11) refers to this reaction by educators as "violated exclusivity," which is the unwarranted reaction of a social group that possesses a valuable commodity to the wider dissemination of the commodity through alternate routes. Inevitably, the group that possesses the commodity characterizes the alternate routes as being marked by lesser standards. It would seem that given the strict academic and administrative protocols of PONSI and their mirroring of higher education standards there would be little resistance to such credit awards. However, because the process is out of the direct control of the college and its faculty, the assessment is perceived as being of lesser quality. Ironically, cooperative education, which incorporates the benefits of experiential learning in off-campus settings, is an accepted and growing program in most colleges because it is supervised by faculty (frequently with far fewer institutional controls on the quality of the program than required by PONSI) and, of course, subsidized by student tuition and fees.

It has been almost a hundred years since Dewey (1938) developed his theory of experience, and fifty years since the advent of the GI Bill and the start of the influx of adults to college campuses, yet the mission, philosophy, and practice of most universities have not kept pace with the significant advances in the assessment of learning. The university has persisted in maintaining its form and structure with only occasional concessions to innovation and change.

However, the recent advances in information technology and the development of the service economy, with its requirement for perpetual or continuous learning, should compel higher education to reassess its mission and philosophy. The university is shifting from an instructional paradigm in which productivity is measured by the amount of contact time between a faculty expert and students to a learning paradigm in which productivity is measured by the assessment of outcomes (Barr and Tagg, 1995). The combination of interactive technology and a shift in philosophy and mission may actually lead to the fulfillment of an earlier promise to increase access to higher education for all segments of society. Enhanced learning through more intense, technology-based interactivity will necessitate the institutionalization of assessment programs.

Programs like National PONSI and CREDIT provide a model to institutions of higher education as these institutions struggle to be more accountable for achieving their outcomes and to establish programs that will meet the needs of an adult population living and working in a turbulent, ever-changing service economy. Adult students will have their educational needs fulfilled one way or another. It is in higher education's best interest to recognize that learning may be acquired in many ways and in many places, and that learning must be acknowledged with awards of appropriate academic credit via sound assessment techniques. If higher education does not make these adjustments, it will be replaced by proprietary universities, which will understand, value, and control the learning enterprise.

Conclusion

National PONSI and CREDIT provide a valuable service to adult college students by assessing the learning they acquired in a noncollegiate program of study. Their policies and procedures are appropriate to higher education, and all assessments are made by qualified faculty. The PONSI approach has its roots in several educational traditions that provide a solid theoretical foundation for the process. Information technology and the advent of a service-dominated economy will make institutions of higher education critically evaluate their missions, philosophy, and practices, or they will be challenged for supremacy in education in the adult market by proprietary organizations. The PONSI approach provides a solid model for higher education to emulate as it seeks to assess noncollegiate sponsored instruction, and it is one piece of a long process of evolution from an instructional paradigm to a learning paradigm.

References

American Council on Education. *Review Preparation Handbook.* Washington, D.C.: American Council on Education/Program on Noncollegiate Sponsored Instruction, 1996a.

American Council on Education. *The National Guide to Educational Credit for Training Programs.* Washington, D.C.: American Council on Education/Program on Noncollegiate Sponsored Instruction, 1996b.

Barr, R. B., and Tagg, J. "From Teaching to Learning: A New Paradigm for Undergraduate Education." *Change,* 1995, 27 (6), 13–25.

Board of Regents of the University of the State of New York. *College Credit Recommendations: The Directory of the National Program on Noncollegiate Sponsored Instruction.* Albany, N.Y.: Board of Regents of the University of the State of New York, 1996.

Carnegie Commission on Higher Education. *Less Time, More Options: Beyond the High School.* New York: McGraw-Hill, 1971a.

Carnegie Commission on Higher Education. *New Students and New Places: Policies for the Future Growth and Development of American Higher Education.* New York: McGraw-Hill, 1971b.

Carnegie Commission on Higher Education. *The Fourth Revolution: Instructional Technology in Higher Education.* New York: McGraw-Hill, 1972.

Commission on Non-Traditional Study. *Diversity by Design.* San Francisco: Jossey-Bass, 1973.

Cremin, L. A. *Popular Education and Its Discontents.* New York: HarperCollins, 1989.

Dewey, J. *Experience and Education.* New York: Collier Books, 1938.

Gamson, Z. F. *Higher Education and the Real World: The Story of CAEL.* Wolfeboro, N.H.: Longwood Academic, 1989.

Knowles, M. S. *The Modern Practice of Adult Education: Andragogy Versus Pedagogy.* New York: Association Press, 1970.

Meyer, P. *Awarding College Credit for Non-College Learning.* San Francisco: Jossey-Bass, 1975.

Rose, A. "Nontraditional Education and the Assessment of Prior Learning." In S. B. Merriam and P. Cunningham (eds.), *The Handbook of Adult and Continuing Education.* San Francisco: Jossey-Bass, 1989.

Willingham, W. "Critical Issues and Basic Requirements." In M. Keeton (ed.), *Experiential Learning, Rationale, and Assessment.* San Francisco: Jossey-Bass, 1976.

RICHARD J. HAMILTON *is vice president of academic affairs at Charter Oak State College in Newington, Connecticut.*

Portfolio-assisted assessment typically follows Western academic assumptions about universal, value-neutral knowledge. It can be significantly strengthened by recognizing that knowledge is always embedded in specific social, cultural, and historical contexts.

Multicultural Approaches to Portfolio Development

Elana Michelson

Prior learning assessment (PLA), which began as a way to serve adult students returning to college after the two world wars, came to be widely utilized in higher education beginning in the late 1960s and early 1970s. As both the need for professional credentials and the desire for meaningful leisure drove increasing numbers of adults back to higher education, a vehicle was needed for recognizing the often considerable college-level knowledge that these adults had gained through a variety of learning experiences—employment, community and organizational activity, and self-study, to name but three. A variety of instruments—including national standardized exams, campus-based "challenge exams" in specific courses, interviews and demonstrations, the generic evaluation of noncollegiate sponsored educational programs such as nursing schools and skilled apprenticeships, and narrative and analytical essays—allowed students to demonstrate college-equivalent knowledge.

By providing a way to translate knowledge gained outside the academy into college credits, PLA both eased the way for individual students and, more generally, changed the relationship between the faculty, students, and the institution. Adult students had to be seen as coproducers of academically credible knowledge rather than as blank slates to be filled in by professors, who were seen as having a monopoly on expertise. This in turn posed new challenges to

While writing this chapter I was all too aware of the historical relationship between white scholars and non-European traditions of learning, in which the appropriation and misuse of knowledge mirrored the appropriation and misuse of people and the land. I have tried very hard not to perpetuate that shameful history. I am deeply indebted to Diane Hill and Banakonda Kennedy-Kish Bell, whose intellectual and spiritual understanding of experiential learning has informed and inspired me.

the staff of academic institutions. Faculty had to learn to evaluate knowledge they had not themselves imparted, and counselors and administrators had to devise new systems for assessing and accrediting students' expertise (Whitaker, 1989; Lamdin, 1997).

In one sense, the recognition of students' college-equivalent knowledge was seen as an act of simple fairness: if experienced adults had gained academically equivalent learning through work, volunteer activity, and independent study, that learning should be formally acknowledged. As PLA advocates repeatedly argued, what one actually knew was more important than where one had happened to learn it. Thus there was no reason why noncollegiate sponsored training should not be evaluated for college credit. PLA was simply one more version of the ways in which students had always demonstrated their college-level learning: essays and term papers, demonstrations, interviews with faculty, and course-specific and standardized exams.

Viewed more broadly, however, PLA was part of a sweeping and multifaceted movement to rewrite the relationship between the university and the larger society. The implementation of PLA was largely concurrent with such trends as "relevance" in education, greater access for underserved populations, joint ventures between colleges and the private sector, and a more inclusive curriculum.

Among these developments, PLA had a special function as a meeting ground between the academic and nonacademic cultures of knowledge. PLA institutionalized the recognition that knowledge gained outside the walls of the academy could be both *credible* and *creditable,* and that knowledge was created through human activity in many places and forms. If it were to serve as a way to bring cultures of knowledge together, however, PLA had to provide more than a simple quantification of knowledge through standardized assessment instruments. A means was required for encouraging dialogue among students, faculty, and institutions and for exploring the role of knowledge in the lives of students and within the academy. Portfolios—that is, collections of extended narrative essays that describe learning experiences, identify the college-level learning gained, and provide appropriate documentation—have served many institutions as that means.

Portfolios and Alternative Views of Knowledge and Knowing

Portfolios work so well in this regard because they require both an extended self-exploration and a probing into the nature of knowledge as organized academically. Proponents argue that both the student and the academy are thereby enriched. On the one hand, students experience themselves as competent learners, they investigate academic expectations and norms, they explore the relationship between their own prior learning and the contours of academic inquiry, and they take control of their own educational needs. On the other hand, PLA provides a counterweight to overly cerebral assumptions about knowledge, brings the fresh air of everyday experience into academic discourse, and contributes to building a more responsive, flexible, and student-centered academy (Mandell and Michelson, 1990).

Thus PLA generally, and portfolio-assisted PLA in particular, has advanced a variety of movements within higher education. Specifically, it has been both cause and effect of programming for a nontraditional college population, it has helped higher education to serve such economic goals as career flexibility and national competitiveness, and it has furthered the academic recognition of knowledge created through diverse experiences and multiple learning styles.

At the same time, however, PLA has developed at a curious distance from equally important innovations in higher education, specifically the movement towards a more inclusive curriculum and the new approaches to knowledge inspired by feminist, antiracist, and postmodernist schools of thought. Portfolio-assisted PLA has largely retained quite conventional disciplinary organizations of knowledge; moreover, the assumptions about knowledge that undergird PLA are quite conservative. In effect, students are asked to emulate the "objective" role of the professional or academic observer. While their knowledge may be rooted in personal experience, it must be detached from subjectivity, emotion, and self-interest in the process of writing the portfolio. Accreditable knowledge must be portrayed as universal and objective—as broad, impartial, and value-free (Michelson, 1996).

As an example of this, let us explore *mothering* as an area of learning. As portfolio-assisted PLA is currently practiced, students' own experience with mothering, even with children with special needs, is not seen as sufficiently extensive or theoretical to establish accreditable learning. To be accreditable, knowledge of mothering must include "objective" knowledge of child psychology, say, or special education that is roughly equivalent to academic or professional expertise. In some ways, of course, this insistence is justifiable; for knowledge to "count" academically, it must have some relationship to a branch of inquiry that exists somewhere within the academy. At the same time, this approach requires knowledge outside of the experience of mothering *per se*. The assumption seems to be that accreditable knowledge is at considerable distance from the subjectivity of concrete social relationships and from the narrowness of personal and family history. Indeed, the questions typically asked in portfolio development exercises—such as What did you *do?* followed by What did you *learn?*—assume that knowledge must be abstracted from its experiential origins in a way that most students find both difficult and artificial. Alternative questions that might capture the immediacy and engagedness of the experiential context—What did you *do?* followed by Why did you do it? What other choices were available? How might it have been done in other circumstances? How were your choices determined by the social context?—are rarely asked.

What is particularly ironic about these requirements is that, far from grounding PLA in state-of-the-art academic thought, they in fact reflect rather outdated notions that have been importantly challenged in contemporary academic thought. In the postmodernist critique of Enlightenment theories of knowledge and in such new interdisciplinary fields as women's studies and cultural studies, the ideal of "disinterested" and "universal" knowledge has been placed within its own historical context and understood as related to power dynamics within society. Scholars have analyzed the victory of male physicians over female midwives, for example, as having less to do with knowledge of birthing (the midwives of the time were *far* more skilled than the doctors) than with the evolving power dynamics of gender and class (Ehrenreich and English, 1978). Similarly, historians of the social sciences have traced the connections between the power dynamics of the field of anthropology and colonialist rule (Clifford and Marcus, 1986).

In effect, contemporary theory argues that no knowledge is ever value free or detached from social relationships. Rather than gaining legitimacy through its claim to abstraction, knowledge should be seen as richer and less error prone to the degree that its social context and power ladenness are understood. Although the ideal of objectivity and abstract knowledge has of course led to many important breakthroughs, it has also served as a way of dismissing the knowledge of those who are outside formal knowledge practices such as science and academia—often women, workers, and non-Europeans (Collins, 1991; Harding, 1991; Minnich, 1990). The separation of "doing" and "learning," for example, although it arguably promotes habits of reflection, is at the same time part of a class structure that values mental over manual labor and legitimates social privilege based on that unequal valuing.

The movement within academia toward a more inclusive curriculum must be seen, in part, in that context. Far from introducing an inexact and dangerous relativism into academic thought, knowledge can be both expanded and corrected through attention to its cultural embeddedness and to the standpoints that arise from the life experience of socially marginalized groups (Harstock, 1983; Harding, 1991).

How, then, would the approach to mothering be altered in accordance with these new approaches to knowledge? First, the reluctance to accredit such knowledge in the first place would be understood as part of a general disinclination to accredit knowledge from the private realm, with all the gender issues that implies, and more generally it would be understood as a devaluing of the kinds of knowledge generated in the course of female lives. Second, alternatives would be found to disciplinary categorizations of knowledge, such as education and psychology, that originate in the division between "actors" and "observers" and that give authority to powerful social institutions and professional coteries that claim the right to investigate, judge, and proscribe based on their possession of "objective" and "dispassionate" knowledge. The alternative approach to knowledge reintegrates the experiencing actor back into the subject matter so that one speaks as an interested, feeling participant, not as an abstract and powerful observer. This approach understands all forms of knowledge as arising from specific social roles and relationships, and thus as value laden, culturally specific, and implicated in social relationships of power and authority.

This alternative view of knowledge can broaden the field within which students can articulate their understanding of mothering, through theoretical frameworks available from their own experience. For example, a number of major feminist texts have explored the disjunction and power dynamics between male expertise and the experience of many women. Adrienne Rich's *Of Woman Born: Motherhood as Experience and Institution* (1976) and Betty Friedan's *The Feminine Mystique* ([1963] 1984), to name but two, have examined motherhood as a social institution, and the kinds of psychological, familial, and societal expectations through which "proper" maternal emotions and actions are defined. Many students have gained equivalent learning based on their reading or by reflecting on what mothers are "supposed" to do and feel compared to the actual experience of motherhood, or more generally, on motherhood as an evolving social institution and social role.

Similarly, students from non-U.S. cultures often understand mothering as a culturally specific practice. They have detailed and highly sophisticated knowledge of how mothering is practiced differently within a variety of nuclear and extended family structures. They have historical and current perspectives on non-Western family traditions, such as the role of "other mothers" in many Africa-based cultures, and they understand the impact of class structure and of patterns of female employment on the practice of mothering. It is important to realize that these stores of knowledge are no less theoretically important than the more entrenched perspectives of education or psychology. They are certainly no less significant within contemporary academic thought. Such approaches have become an important venue through which the experience of students has emerged as the stuff of serious academic inquiry. How ironic that PLA practice has lagged behind.

Prior Learning Assessment and the Cultural Dimensions of Knowledge

There are a number of reasons, it seems to me, why PLA practices have largely been isolated from these theoretical developments. First, in most institutions PLA has developed in the face of powerful conservative opposition. Thus the politics of PLA advocacy have spurred its advocates to emphasize how *little* PLA challenges traditional academic power arrangements or upsets traditional academic conceptualizations. Second, the division of academic labor between scholarship and student services tends to isolate PLA advocates from exciting new approaches. Portfolio-assisted PLA is a labor-intensive venture. Its proponents tend to be all-too-busy practitioners for whom the theories emerging on the other end of campus can appear a world away.

Perhaps most significant, there has been a curious divide between the movement for academic programming to serve adults and the movement toward a multicultural and woman-friendly academy. Mainstream North American adult education tends to view age as the single significant social category. We speak of "the" adult learner as if human experience is not also molded by gender, class, and race. Thus, aspects of PLA practice that arguably disadvantage women—the relatively low credit awards for traditional "women's work" such as nursing, for example—are not engaged as explicitly feminist issues. Similarly, we rarely link the collective experience of cultural and ethnic groups as a source of accreditable learning to the struggle for a culturally inclusive academy.

The need for PLA to recognize the cultural component of knowledge has already been institutionalized in a number of places.

The Maori. According to PLA policies in New Zealand, the relationship of knowledge to ethnicity must be taken into account. New Zealand's system for PLA is professionally rather than academically based, but its attention to multiculturalism and its recognition of Maori traditions of learning make it an important case in point.

The inclusion of Maori dimensions of learning takes a number of forms. First, New Zealand recognizes that knowledge in such areas as management is never culturally neutral. While some generic managerial skills no doubt exist, Maori management practices reflect both a different social structure and different values concerning social relationships, the environment, and the exercise of leadership, and PLA must take account of approaches that are specific to Maori communities. Standards have been framed accordingly:

> People credited with this unit standard are able to analyze organizational and job structures for *tribal* and *sub-tribal* organizations, urban Maori authorities and other selected Maori organizations by incorporating collective ownership and responsibility, *genealogy, lineage, and family structure; self-determination; respect for elders; ceremony; tribal, extended family,* inter-generational responsibility; *personal authority; spirituality; custom*; and other selected concepts into the structures [New Zealand Qualifications Authority, n.d.][1]

Specific Maori standards are being developed in fishing and forestry, management and administration, and such traditional skills as carving and weaving. In addition, Maori components are being written into national qualifications standards in areas such as health care, social work, and the law (New Zealand Qualifications Authority, n.d.). Moreover, even outside of Maori communities, knowledge of the differences between European and Maori cultures is understood to be needed by businesses and organizations if managers are to be effective (Jefferies and Johns, 1995). Again, the standards reflect this:

> People credited with this unit standard are able to analyse and explain strategies for marketing to Maori clients. They are able to analyse and explain specific attributes of Maori segments of the selected market or markets. They are able to analyse and identify Maori *interests* and Maori *customs* which explain undesirable attitudes towards certain products and promotions which may be culturally offensive to Maori. They are able to analyse and explain marketing strategies which are grounded in Maori interests and reflect Maori perspectives on the

world. They are able to design strategies for marketing to Maori clients [New Zealand Qualifications Authority, n.d.].

Second, New Zealand has recognized that the standards by which knowledge is judged are themselves culturally specific and that Maori beliefs about knowledge are in some cases in opposition to Western academic and professional beliefs. Maori traditions of learning hold that knowledge is collectively owned by the community and that individual knowledge must be considered within a context of interdependence, cooperation, and mutual accountability. Similarly, the Maori teach that learning cannot be evaluated without attention to its ethical and religious dimensions. Even technical skills such as weaving and carving have their spiritual component, and no knowledge can be assessed without attention to its socially responsible use (Benton, Benton, Swindells, and Chrisp, n.d.).

Finally, New Zealand has recognized that Maori people have long had their own assessment structures for traditional skills, such as carving. Assessment procedures are being developed, therefore, that include the participation of Maori educators and that involve the Maoris' own internal systems for assessment of Maori skills. The implication, of course, is that so-called mainstream professional and academic experts cannot have the exclusive right to assess learning, and that assessment policies must embrace the notion of shared authority based on complementary expertise.

First Nations Technical Institute. Even with this impressive degree of cultural sensitivity, the highly standardized, preset criteria for PLA in New Zealand and the failure to use portfolios as a vehicle for assessment hamper the richness of learning that can be assessed, whether of Maori or European cultural roots. At the First Nations Technical Institute (FNTI) in Canada, however, a program has been developed that uses portfolio development to explore a wide range of individual and collective learning. The program is exciting both because of its utilization of non-European theories of knowledge and because of its ability to capture the cognitive, emotional, and spiritual nuances of prior learning.

FNTI is an educational institution located on the Tyendinaga Mohawk territory in southeastern Ontario. It offers programs in welfare administration, child and family Services, adult literacy, recreation leadership, small business management, and aerospace technology. A partnership with Loyalist College allows students in human service fields to apply for credit for prior learning and to earn diplomas that are the equivalent of U.S. associate degrees.

FNTI's approach to experiential learning is increasingly grounded in aboriginal[2] traditions and history and has been collectively developed by four members of the faculty: Mohawk educators Diane Hill and Robert Antone, and Ojibwa Midewan educators Banakonda Kennedy-Kish Bell and James Dumont. According to their approach, the first peoples of North America have a collective experience of "ethnostress" caused by violent conquest leading to cultural and economic dislocation. That dislocation continues to disrupt collective and personal identity, producing such social problems as alcohol dependency, child abuse, and chronic unemployment, and contributing to numerous psychic and intellectual scars that interfere with the ability to learn (Hill, 1995).

Thus portfolio development takes place within a context in which both personal healing and cultural renewal are educational goals. When constructing a portfolio of past experiences, individual students inevitably confront pain arising from symptoms of ethnostress. "First we must go back through our lives and keep putting down our burdens. Then we can come forward again and pick them back up. Looking this second time we can see them not as failures and hardships but as learning" (Bell, 1997). In addition, the examination of values and experience must address the problem of incomplete cultural assimilation and the resultant confusion between aboriginal and Euro-Canadian values. Portfolios at FNTI therefore serve a variety of academic and cultural purposes. As the guidelines for students explain: "At FNTI, prior learning assessment is used as a multi-purpose educational tool. Once completed, the portfolio will allow you to compare not only previously acquired competencies (knowledge and skills) with current program requirements and learning outcomes, but also, your knowledge, skills, attitudes, and feelings related to your cultural heritage, beliefs, and practices" (Hill, 1995, p. 68).

As "documented portraits," FNTI portfolios both express the learning of individuals and serve as a mirror to the community of its own experience. Appropriately, given their cultural and historical setting, they are acts of "storytelling" (Hill, 1995, p. 62) in the deepest sense of the term.

The approach to prior learning that is structured into FNTI's portfolio development rests on two tenets of aboriginal teachings that differ markedly from European traditions of knowledge. First, rather than assuming that learning is essentially a cognitive process, portfolio development at FNTI is grounded in aboriginal perspectives about knowledge that put the spirit, not the head, at the core. "Humans are physical beings endowed with mind and heart (emotions) and empowered by spirit" (Hill, 1995, p. 43). Learning is a holistic process that requires the spiritual, intellectual, emotional, and physical aspects of self.

The difference between this approach and that of the dominant North American approach can be seen if we compare FNTI's learning cycle with that of David Kolb. According to Kolb (1984), as the individual passes through the steps of the learning cycle—concrete experience, observation and reflection, abstract concepts and generalization, and active experimentation—the mind accesses information about the world and uses that information to produce learning. The body functions essentially as sensate medium and testing instrument, while the emotions and the spirit do not participate at all. As is consistent with European-derived views of knowledge, learning is a product of the mind alone.

In the learning cycle used at FNTI, spirit, mind, heart, and body (that is, intuition, cognitive knowledge, emotions, and material skills) all serve as agents of forms of learning. As in Kolb, these translate into various preferred learning styles. More important, all four must be present for any complete learning to take place. (See Figure 4.1.) Theoretical understanding must be joined both to feelings and to active physical engagement with the world, and all must be grounded within the spirit-based insight and calling through which human beings experience and come to know (B. K-K. Bell, personal communication with author, April 16, 1997; Bell and Conlon, 1996; D. Hill, personal communication with author, February 12, 1997).

The second tenet of aboriginal thought that distinguishes FNTI's approach is the assumed relationship of the individual to others and to the world as a whole. In most North American institutions, approaches to lifelong learning are based on individualism and humanistic psychology and see psychic and intellectual growth as a moving away from others. Malcolm Knowles's ([1973] 1990) use of Carl Rogers's and Abraham Maslow's theories is a case in point. Because the goal of learning is self-actualization, it requires a passage from passivity and reactiveness to activity and autonomy. The choice is always between dependence and independence: "I have yet to find the individual who, when

Figure 4.1. Learning Cycle Developed by Banakonda Bell for Use at FNTI

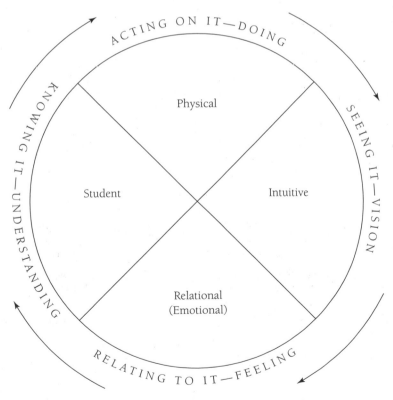

Source: Bell and Conlon, 1996. Used with permission.

he [sic] examines his situation deeply, . . . deliberately chooses dependence, deliberately chooses to have the integrated direction of himself undertaken by another" (Rogers, quoted in Knowles, [1973] 1990, p. 42).

At FNTI, the approach to lifelong learning is not based on this apparent choice between independence or dependence. Rather, it is rooted in the notion of interdependence and collective responsibility. The spiritual basis of education includes the quest for balance: individual choice is important, but it must be made with regard for what is best for others, both in the present and, as aboriginal teaching requires, seven generations ahead (Hill, 1995). One's life evolves within structures of knowledge that are both personal and collective, grounded both in the uniqueness of an individual destiny and in the collective memories, struggles, and fulfillments of particular historical times (B. K-K. Bell, personal communication with author, April 16, 1997). Knowledge thus bears the responsibility for human and environmental well-being; it is measured in relational rather than individual proficiency.

Thus, rather than seeing lifelong learning in terms of ever-greater autonomy, FNTI defines it in terms of connectedness to larger and larger circles of existence. Situating oneself experientially means placing oneself within "ever-expanding circles of involvement and interaction," moving from "'standing within yourself' to interacting with others within your family, extended family, clan, community, nation, confederacy, the environment and world beyond . . ." (Hill, 1995, p. 70). One whole section of the portfolio is therefore structured according to those ever-expanding circles, as students repeat the cycle of performance within ever-larger human and ecological relationships.

These cycles, in turn, form the basis for FNTI's definition of competence. Competence is defined holistically as "the development of the whole person within the total environment," not only to promote the survival for all living things but also "to achieve a life of quality beyond survival, . . . living one's life with meaning, purpose, and a profound thankfulness" (Hill, 1995, pp. 34–35). Competence therefore includes the ability to function in multiple roles, the knowledge and skills relative to social context and social history, strategies for intervention based on an understanding of family and community patterns, personal and interpersonal healing and wellness, the design of and participation in models of social action for ecological well-being, and the creation of shared wealth based on aboriginal beliefs.

As an aid to students in their portfolio development, FNTI faculty members Robert Antone and James Dumont have developed a Competency and Performance Model for each of the ever-expanding cycles of relationship. Under "Experiencing One's Self in the Cultural Reality of an Aboriginal Community," for example, performance standards include the following:

a. Able to articulate personal issues and feelings about being a part of an aboriginal community.
b. Able to begin to struggle with the healing of aboriginal community issues and its recovery from the effects of ethnostress and western cultural conditioning.

c. Able to understand internal community conflict and the aspects of one's aboriginal community which require change and can identify the relating patterns which either hinder or help the building of relationships.

d. Able to describe a plan of care related to a lifelong program of healing to improve and to strengthen relationships within one's aboriginal community [Hill, 1995, p. 98].

As mentioned previously, Loyalist College functions as FNTI's accrediting partner in the human service fields. Loyalist's support for FNTI has required a willingness to move beyond its own assumptions and to acknowledge the validity of alternative approaches to learning and curriculum. This alone makes it an important model for other educational institutions, as does its determination to engage with local communities and to mediate between those communities and the educational powers that be (R. Conlon and P. Zakos, personal communication with author, February 12, 1997). However, although its partnership with FNTI continues to develop, Loyalist is an academically traditional institution governed by the Ministry of Education and Training. Portfolios that are used as the basis for credit awards must meet imposed definitions of *competence* as well as FNTI's definitions. The section of students' portfolios that is devoted to application for credit therefore uses a narrow definition of competence as "the things you know how to do" (Hill, 1995, p. 75). Students are required to develop a series of "competency statements" that utilize both "task analysis" and "learning analysis" and that follow the usual logic of portfolio development, namely, they distinguish between what students have done and what they have learned.

There is of course nothing wrong with having students reflect on and identify their professional skills and underlying knowledge. But in this section of the portfolio, the richness of FNTI's approach to portfolios threatens to fall away. In the translation of their prior learning into Loyalist College credits, the depth of students' social, cultural, political, and historical learning is minimized. Accreditable knowledge narrows to a specific professional expertise.

This is especially troublesome given the curricular focus on community and human services. The FNTI competencies detailed earlier speak profoundly to strategies for personal and community healing that are appropriate in aboriginal communities; one need hardly be a radical multiculturalist to argue that such competencies are relevant to a social work degree. Arguably, a knowledge of the local culture and of the history of economic and social dislocation is an important and academically valid aspect of a social worker's education, and any curriculum attuned to cultural realities might well include such material among its offerings or else strongly encourage students to do course work in departments of community studies or anthropology. But Loyalist's curriculum, based on the assumption that academic training is generic and that accreditable knowledge is universal and disembodied, has no such curricular offerings. The knowledge of aboriginal culture, history, and social problems that would be crucial to a more culturally aware and interdisciplinary curriculum is not currently recognized as "college equivalent."

Part of the difficulty is that the system within which Loyalist operates currently requires that assessable credit should match specific courses that happen to be offered in that particular institution. Thus, learning must not only be generally college-level, but it must also match the often-arbitrary contours of a specific course in a specific academic department and discipline. This is often an enormous disadvantage to students whose learning derives from the workplace and the community, not only at FNTI but in most PLA-granting institutions in North America.

Conclusion

I would argue, however, that the problem runs much deeper. The portfolios produced at FNTI have many facets. To be sure, they are compilations of professional knowledge and skill, but they are also chronicles of courage and wisdom that reverberate historically for many social groups, not only aboriginal North Americans but also others with a common history of cultural and economic struggle and a rich wellspring of values and beliefs. They cannot currently be assessed for college credit because PLA practice overall does not yet recognize such things as accreditable learning. We have not yet sufficiently overcome a tradition that sees knowledge as detached from collective human memories and purpose. We continue to define knowledge as the product of thought alone rather than as the combined effect of thought, pain, joy, activity, remembrance, and vision. We continue to insist that accreditable knowledge be "universal," as if all human knowledge did not arise within specific histories.

Portfolio development at FNTI uniquely reflects not only aboriginal teachings about knowledge but also the new understandings about knowledge that are emerging from the contemporary academy: that knowledge is the product of the interaction of human beings within specific social and historical settings, that knowledge always has a value-laden component, and that the experience of life in marginalized social categories is an important corrective to more privileged perspectives. FNTI's approach to portfolio development thus allows us to expand assessable prior learning to include the understandings that students have of historical struggles and triumphs, the often painful and unequal interactions between dominant and marginalized groups, the differences among belief systems and why they matter, the never-only-individual sustaining of existence within human communities.

Endnotes

1. The italicized portions of this and the following quotation are written in Maori in the New Zealand Qualifications Authority Standards. I am indebted to Richard Benton for these translations.

2. I have used the term *aboriginal* to conform with the preferred usage among First Nations peoples in Canada, rather than the term *native,* which is used more often in the United States.

References

Bell, B. K-K., and Conlon, R. "The FNTI Approach to Prior Learning." Paper presented at the Canadian Association for Prior Learning Assessment Conference, Belleville, Ontario, May 1996.

Benton, N., Benton, R., Swindells, J., and Chrisp, T. *The Unbroken Thread: Maori Learning and the National Qualifications Framework*. Wellington: New Zealand Council for Educational Research, n.d.

Clifford, J., and Marcus, G. E. (eds.). *Writing Culture: The Poetics and Politics of Ethnography*. Berkeley: University of California Press, 1986.

Collins, P. H. *Black Feminist Thought: Knowledge, Consciousness, and the Politics of Empowerment*. New York: Routledge, 1991.

Ehrenreich, B., and English, D. *For Her Own Good: 150 Years of Experts' Advice to Women*. New York: Anchor Books, 1978.

Friedan, B. *The Feminine Mystique*. New York: Dell, 1984. (Originally published 1963.)

Harding, S. *Whose Science? Whose Knowledge? Thinking from Women's Lives*. Ithaca, N.Y.: Cornell University Press, 1991.

Harstock, N. "The Feminist Standpoint: Developing the Grounds for a Specifically Feminist Historical Materialism." In S. Harding and M. Hintikka (eds.), *Discovering Reality: Feminist Perspectives on Epistemology, Methodology, and Philosophy of Science*. Dordrecht/Boston: Reidel, 1983.

Hill, D. *Aboriginal Access to Post-Secondary Education: Prior Learning Assessment and Its Use with Aboriginal Programs of Learning*. Desoronto, Ontario: First Nations Technical Institute, 1995.

Jefferies, R., and Johns, H. *Maori Business, Administration, and Finance Whakaruruhau: Unit Standards Development Scoping Report*. Wellington: New Zealand Qualifications Authority, 1995.

Knowles, M. *The Adult Learner: A Neglected Species*. Houston, Tex.: Gulf, 1990. (Originally published 1973.)

Kolb, D. *Experiential Learning: Experience as the Source of Learning and Development*. Englewood Cliffs, N.J.: Prentice Hall, 1984.

Lamdin, L. *Earn College Credit for What You Know*. (3rd ed.) Chicago: Council for Adult and Experiential Learning, 1997.

Mandell, A., and Michelson, E. *Portfolio Development and Adult Learning: Purposes and Strategies*. Chicago: Council for Adult and Experiential Learning, 1990.

Michelson, E. "Beyond Galileo's Telescope: Situated Knowledge and the Assessment of Experiential Learning." *Adult Education Quarterly*, 1996, 46 (4), 185–196.

Minnich, E. *Transforming Knowledge*. Philadelphia: Temple University Press, 1990.

New Zealand Qualifications Authority. *Whaia Te Iti Kahurangi [In Pursuit of Excellence]: Maori and Qualifications*. Wellington: New Zealand Qualifications Authority, n.d.

Rich, A. *Of Woman Born: Motherhood as Experience and Institution*. New York: Norton, 1976.

Whitaker, U. *Assessing Learning: Standards, Principles, and Procedures*. Chicago: Council for Adult and Experiential Learning, 1989.

ELANA MICHELSON is associate professor at Empire State College, State University of New York.

An integrated framework for outcomes assessment is discussed.
Multiple measures of multiple goals, aligned with mission,
culture, objectives, and environment, are shared.

A Model for Developing an Outcomes Assessment Plan: The Regents College Outcomes Assessment Framework

Paula E. Peinovich, Mitchell S. Nesler, Todd S. Thomas

Outcomes assessment is a hot topic in higher education. Accrediting bodies have mandated that institutions develop formal assessment plans to determine whether students are meeting intended outcomes. State legislatures are demanding proof that public dollars invested in higher education are yielding public benefits. Even President Clinton, in his 1997 inaugural address, spoke of increasing accountability in higher education. For Regents College of the University of the State of New York, outcomes assessment is the very foundation on which the institution was built more than twenty-five years ago, before the concept of value-added higher education had even been considered. Throughout its history the college has continued to refine and reevaluate its outcomes assessment framework, which is based on a multiple measures approach to evaluating institutional effectiveness.

Regents College was founded by the New York State Board of Regents in 1971 as an outcomes-based examining institution following the historic model of the University of London External Programme. Its mission is to create access to higher education for adult learners who face barriers of time, place, and educational background, as well as for those who have historically been underserved by the higher education community.

Today Regents College serves 60,000 adult learners annually through its degree and assessment programs. During its first twenty-five years, almost 80,000 adult learners have graduated from the institution. The average age of the learners is forty, and they come from every state in the union and from many countries around the globe. Twenty-three percent are from historically underrepresented populations, and the student body is equally balanced between genders. The college offers twenty-eight degree programs in four academic divisions: business, liberal arts, nursing, and technology. It believes that everyone should have an equal chance to *pursue* a Regents College degree, although once adult learners have enrolled they must *earn* their degrees by demonstrating that they have met the outcomes specified by faculty.

At its founding, Regents College was what today would be called a *virtual university*. It emerged when adult learners were still in the minority among college goers, and when they had few choices. Twenty-five years later, much has changed for adult learners, yet much has remained the same. There are more programs and choices, and adults have grown to be the majority of students in higher education today (National Center for Education Statistics, 1995). The increasing availability of technology and the growing use of the Internet for educational endeavors has removed some of the barriers of time and place. Yet one thing has remained constant and that is the belief that unless a learner has sat in an institution's classroom, be it made of bricks and mortar or ethernet, she or he has not really learned. From an institutional perspective, the academic residency requirement is quite attractive. It ensures fiscal health by filling classrooms and gives some degree of quality assurance to those charged with evaluating academic quality; after all, passing grades on courses taught by local faculty are easily understood direct assessments of successful course outcomes. From the perspective of adult learners, however, academic residency requirements are often formidable barriers to earning their college degrees.

The idea of academic residency still dominates traditional institutions' academic policies. Even the growing number of virtual universities protect their core business by requiring academic residency, offering their virtuality only in time and space. By failing to recognize that learning occurs outside of their own institutions, they stop short of actually being virtual learning institutions. The concept of the virtual university has become tied up in the public mind with technology instead of with learning. While the technological infrastructure of our society grows rapidly, the concept of a learning infrastructure is only dimly understood. A truly virtual university would consider an adult learner's whole life the university, and the most important function of a truly virtual university would be to assess and authenticate the learning of a lifetime. It is in this sense that Regents College is the nation's first virtual university. Its programs grow out of an outcomes framework based on two fundamental beliefs:

• What one knows is more important than where one learned it.
• There are a variety of sound methods by which to assess a person's knowledge.

Regents College requires no academic residency; this single academic policy makes it virtual and sets it apart from all other institutions. The college's belief that knowledge is important regardless of its source and its use of a range of methods to measure the outcomes of its curriculum have led the college to believe that its degrees represent the lifelong learning of its graduates.

The Regents College Outcomes Framework

In addition to the fundamental beliefs listed earlier, the Regents College outcomes framework includes a philosophy of the college's curriculum, outcomes statements, a heuristic framework for learning, assessment tools, an assessment environment, validation procedures, and a longitudinal assessment of graduate outcomes. The framework underpins all the direct assessments of student learning done at the college, as well as the college's recognition of learning that has been assessed by others within the context of the quality assurance framework provided by regional accreditation, and within the context of the framework provided by the American Council on Education to determine the equivalency of formal learning acquired in the military, business, industry, and the professions to that acquired at institutions of higher education.

Outcomes Assessment Goals. As a prelude to developing an outcomes assessment plan, an institution and its faculty must determine the goals they wish to reach through whatever measures they select. The following goals inform Regents College's outcomes assessment:

1. Students have achieved course outcomes, as required by faculty, for each degree program.
2. Curricula and the outcomes statements of the curricula are current.
3. Curricula (including general education requirements) are effective at achieving stated outcomes.
4. Curricula are equivalent to those offered at traditional institutions.
5. Students have achieved general education outcomes, as stated by faculty.
6. The general education outcomes of Regents College graduates are equivalent to those achieved by graduates of traditional institutions.
7. Students have met program outcomes, as stated by faculty.
8. Program outcomes are equivalent to those achieved by graduates of traditional institutions.
9. The institution is effective in assisting students from all demographic groups to complete their degrees.
10. The programs are creating access for individuals from a diversity of backgrounds, in accordance with the college's mission.
11. Student demographics, enrollment patterns and behaviors, academic characteristics, and performance of graduates have patterns of commonality and differences that result in variable course and program outcomes.
12. Students are satisfied with their programs and with student services.

Curriculum and Outcomes Evaluation. The philosophy of the Regents College curriculum is that undergraduate education seeks to expand·students' understanding from the limitations of individual experience to a full, rich understanding of the complexity of existence. Further, it endeavors to encourage individuals to attain their highest possible level of accomplishment.

Following this philosophy, the faculty of Regents College developed outcomes statements for general education that all students in all programs must meet, and outcomes statements for each degree program. The Regents College general education outcome statements and program outcome statements serve as the basis for the outcome assessment framework. These statements do not remain static but are revisited periodically by faculty to assure their currency. Just as the curriculum changes and evolves, so do an institution's outcome statements need to be updated as the external environment changes. In all cases, the outcomes statements are measurable and determine the requirements of the curriculum. For instance, the faculty expects that the general education curriculum design will ensure that each graduate of Regents College will be able to

1. Read analytically and critically in a range of fields.
2. Write clear, grammatical, and effective prose.
3. Think critically in making judgments and identifying and posing solutions to problems.
4. Develop cohesive arguments using appropriate supporting evidence.
5. Interpret events using more than one perspective, such as historical, economic, biological, social, and global.
6. Explain the role of culture in shaping diverse societies.
7. Identify elements of artistic and creative expression.
8. Apply knowledge of mathematics and the natural sciences in different contexts.
9. Demonstrate an awareness of the ethical implications of actions.

In addition, the faculty have developed outcomes statements for each concentration offered.

The college measures the effectiveness of its general education requirements by administering American College Testing's College Outcome Measures Program (COMP) examination to a representative sample of graduating seniors every three years. This examination series measures graduates' ability to think critically and make judgments and inferences after being exposed to stimulus information. A writing assessment also allows for the assessment of students' ability to organize a persuasive written message. The COMP examinations have a twenty-year history and have been administered to more than 500,000 students at more than seven hundred colleges in the United States (American College Testing, 1992, 1995).

The exams were developed based on a review of general education philosophy statements at numerous colleges and universities and on the assumption that general education coursework should provide students with knowledge and skills that assist their functioning in society (American College Testing, 1995). Despite this assumption, COMP scores do not correlate with age (Forrest and Steele, 1982), which suggests that the tests do not measure maturation but instead measure the effectiveness of an institution's general education core. These examinations demonstrate for Regents College students the integrated learning often achieved through a capstone experience at campus-based institutions (either a course, internship, or senior thesis) and provide a national, standardized measure against which Regents College graduates can be compared. Solid performance on the examinations by graduating seniors indicates that by fulfilling the general education requirements Regents College students are able to integrate their learning from across the arts and sciences into a holistic framework and apply this learning in many contexts.

The use of the COMP examinations represents the use of an aggregate assessment of students' learning to measure the effectiveness of the general education program rather than the effectiveness of each learner. Hence the assessment is a formative one (carried out at the end of each course), measuring the program within the context of continuous improvement. Students do not receive credit for taking the COMP examination; it is a requirement only for a sample of students. The examination process ensures that the degree requirements actually achieve the stated outcomes. This use of assessment further points out that direct assessment of student learning can have two quite different objectives: either it can evaluate the learner's achievement, in either a formative or a summative (at the end of the program) context, or it can evaluate the program's effectiveness, in either a formative or a summative context. A robust outcomes framework should include both formative and summative objectives for both programs and learners, to ensure that learners are meeting the requirements and that the requirements are achieving the stated outcomes.

The Heuristic Framework. The heuristic framework that Regents College has adopted to inform the direct assessment of student learning is Bloom's (1956) Taxonomy of Learning. This familiar and widely accepted taxonomy states that cognitive activity takes place at the levels of knowledge, comprehension, application, analysis, synthesis, and evaluation. Regents College assessments, regardless of their methodology, measure cognitive activity in all areas of the taxonomy. Any heuristic device can be adopted to inform the assessment of students, but it is important that a guiding framework be used to ensure that both lower-order and higher-order processes are assessed, particularly if program outcomes call for knowledge, comprehension, application, and integrative thought processes.

Assessment Tools. There are a wide range of tools available upon which to build an assessment program. These include written examinations, performance examinations, oral examinations, and portfolios as sources of academic credit to document learning. In addition, focus groups, surveys, and interviews serve as sources of information about institutional effectiveness. Management information reports from the institutional database can be used to evaluate and track many issues, such as the enrollment management performance of the institution, especially related to recruitment and retention.

The Regents College Outcomes framework is integrated and seeks multiple sources of information on which to base judgments about the success of the institution in meeting its assessment goals (Cook and Campbell, 1979). Each of the twelve goals is measured using several different tools, and some tools are used to provide assessment information relevant to several goals. For instance, the ACT COMP assessment is used to determine the effectiveness of the general education curriculum, as well as the equivalency of the outcomes of studying general education at Regents College to studying general education at traditional institutions. The equivalency of general education outcomes is also measured through employer surveys, graduate school advisor surveys, and the graduates' self-reported assessments of their own accomplishments. Information from multiple sources can then be reviewed to give a fuller picture of the extent to which the institution is accomplishing its assessment goals.

Regents College directly measures student learning in individual courses through its standardized assessments and through individualized assessment processes. Standardized methods include Regents College Examinations, a battery of examinations developed by panels of faculty from across the United States. The standards of these tests are set by norming them against groups of students who have just completed a course in the content area covered by the examination. These standardized examinations include multiple choice tests, extended response tests (essays), and mixed-format examinations.

Regents College also offers standardized performance examinations in its nursing programs; these are criterion-referenced examinations administered individually to student nurses in both real-time and simulated hospital settings (Regents College, 1997). They are graded by highly trained objective faculty assessors following specific protocols based on criteria of performance that grow out of the outcomes statements for the nursing program. They measure students' clinical skills in nursing at the program level, and require students to demonstrate the integration of their learning from all other requirements of the program. They are high-stakes, summative assessments because they are used to make decisions about a student nurse's ability to practice safely as a first-day graduate. The passing rate for Regents College first-time takers of the National Council of State Boards of Nursing Registered Licensure Examination (NCLEX-RN) has traditionally been higher than the national average for similar programs, thus providing a standardized outcome measure of the effectiveness of the Regents nursing curriculum (Nesler, Hanner, Lettus, and Melburg, 1995). When changes were observed in the NCLEX passing rate for Regents College nursing graduates, changes were made to curricular requirements by the nursing faculty, thus demonstrating that a summative assessment for learners can be a formative one for faculty as they evaluate the curriculum.

Regents College also offers two kinds of individualized assessment: special assessment and portfolio-based assessment. Special assessment is an individualized examination of a student by two faculty members from the same academic discipline. It takes place during a single day, usually at Regents College in Albany. The faculty examine the student in a variety of ways that are determined by the structure of the discipline that is being measured. Methods include direct oral examination, performance assessment (for instance, in the performing arts or in laboratory sciences), portfolio assessment (for instance, in visual arts, journalism, or computer programming), and written examinations (for instance, in mathematics and engineering technology). Both faculty examiners must agree on the award of credit; in case of a disagreement, a third faculty member is called in to examine the student using the same protocols and covering the same topics.

Regents College also offers portfolio assessment to students who have achieved college-level learning in disciplines for which there are no standardized examinations but for which they can produce substantive documentation that the learning has occurred. Students prepare portfolios that describe and document their learning, following standard protocols. The portfolios are evaluated by faculty members from the discipline of the learning described. Faculty assessors for both special assessment and portfolio assessment are trained to recognize that credit should be awarded for learning and not for experience per se, that the college credit is for college-level learning, and that it is balanced between theory and application, following Bloom's taxonomy.

The Assessment Environment. Not only the outcomes to be measured and the objectives of the assessment but also the assessment environment within which an assessment tool is to be used will determine which tool is the most valid and reliable for a task. For instance, if a learner's knowledge base is to be assessed at a single point in time in a distance education program such as Regents College, a much greater stake is placed in the validity and reliability of the assessment instrument and in the integrity of the administration of the assessment. If, conversely, a learner is to be assessed in a classroom context, where the faculty member has a number of assessments, papers, and qualitative information from class discussion with the student on which to base the summative assessment of awarding credit and a grade, each instrument does not have to stand the same rigorous tests of validity and reliability as would instruments used in a single-measure environment. The multiple measures taken for Regents College students across each of their curricula will, when taken in sum, assure the meaningfulness of the degree awarded.

Validation Procedures. The final part of any outcomes framework is the benchmarking or validation of the assessment instruments themselves to assure that they are both truthful and consistent. There are a number of benchmarking processes that can be used to establish the reliability and validity of the instruments. Although large-scale norming and standard setting are requisites for all instruments used in a single-measure assessment environment, a number of other benchmarking processes are accessible to any faculty member, academic department, or institution to enhance the quality of the assessment program. Methods could include content-validity studies as simple as surveying a representative group of external faculty about the content they cover in their curriculum. Construct, content, and discriminant validity can be ensured by using panels of subject-matter experts to develop assessment instruments, by using external validators to review the representative nature of the content of the instruments, by using external examiners to conduct additional assessments of the learner, and by using criterion group (expert and novice) test takers to determine an instrument's ability to discriminate between those who have mastered the content and those who have not. Regents College uses all of these validation processes because it operates almost exclusively within a single-measure assessment environment and, further, operates at a distance from its students. Assessment processes must be continually evaluated to assure their validity and reliability, and to ensure the integrity of the college's degrees (Regents College, 1995).

Longitudinal Assessment of Graduate Outcomes. The final step in the Regents College outcomes framework is the longitudinal tracking of graduates. Students are surveyed shortly after graduation to assess their perceptions of the Regents College experience, their opinions on the quality of service, their immediate plans, and other issues that are associated with the immediate impact of receiving a degree. Data obtained from the postgraduation surveys are analyzed with rich information available on the college's student database, so that following an enrollment management model graduate outcomes can be assessed in light of academic performance and demographic information collected upon enrollment. Both cross-sectional and longitudinal studies are conducted with graduates. Multiple methods allow the college to make inferences about graduates' progress. The impact of earning a Regents College degree is measured relative to the importance of various motivating factors. Baseline data on such elements as income, job progression, and plans for graduate study are collected at this point.

Several years after graduation, each graduate receives another, more comprehensive survey. That instrument focuses on professional development, civic contribution, social integration, efficacy as lifelong learners, self-assessment of achievements in meeting general education outcomes, and critical thinking. Through surveys of their graduate faculty and of employers, the college validates the graduates' reports of their own accomplishments with respect to certain learning outcomes typically evidenced in graduate school or the workplace, such as ethical behavior, communication skills, and the application and integration of knowledge.

Using the Framework

The Regents College outcomes framework supports the academic integrity of a large, virtual institution. But an outcomes framework such as the one described here is equally effective as an organizing principle for any kind of institution. Good assessment plans include multiple measures, some standardized and some individualized, and a variety of assessment tools. Most important, good assessment plans fit the institutional mission and academic goals of the faculty who develop them. All assessment tools, be they multiple-choice examinations or oral defenses of doctoral dissertations, can measure cognitive activity along the entire range of Bloom's taxonomy. A multiple-choice examination can measure an individual's ability to evaluate (a highest-order cognitive operation), just as an essay examination can measure an individual's ability to recall knowledge (lowest-order cognitive activity). It all depends on the beliefs, philosophy, goals, outcomes, and assessment environment of the institution, and on the development or selection of appropriate measures.

All the elements of an outcomes framework are within easy reach of any institution: faculty have assumptions about learning on which they base their curriculum, desired outcomes that graduates should attain can be articulated by faculty, and both formative and summative assessments can be built into the academic requirements.

The process of developing an outcomes framework can be enriching and enlightening for a college faculty as they come together to articulate clearly the outcomes they expect of the curriculum; to state the objectives they are pursuing through different formative and summative assessments; to define their beliefs about cognitive activity; to affirm that the assessment environment at the institution is based on multiple qualitative and quantitative measures; to list all the assessment tools that are in use at the institution, so that faculty can learn various methods and approaches from one another; and to begin to benchmark those assessment tools.

For instance, if an institution required a senior thesis as a capstone assessment, a faculty group could develop a grading guide that all faculty would use to grade senior theses; even if the thesis were given a pass/fail grade, an agreed-upon set of expectations that each passing thesis must meet would greatly strengthen the consistency of the entire academic program. Using such a guide consistently across academic departments to identify students' strengths and weaknesses would also be an excellent way to conduct formative evaluation of the academic program for the purpose of continuous improvement. To enhance the validity and reliability of the assessment process for the senior thesis, the institution could also have more than one faculty member, or an external examiner, read each student's thesis.

Creating an outcomes framework that includes explicit statements about the curriculum and its expected outcomes does not take away from a faculty's academic freedom, nor does it impose assessment processes that do not match the culture, objectives, and assessment environment of any institution. Rather, an explicit framework contributes to the institution's ability to improve its programs continuously and ensure that the outcomes of those programs are achieved by all of its graduates.

References

American College Testing, Inc. *College Outcome Measures Program: Clarifying and Assessing General Education Outcomes of College. Technical Report 1982–1991.* Iowa City, IA: American College Testing, Inc., 1992.

American College Testing, Inc. *College Outcome Measures Program: Technical Report, Appendix C.* Iowa City, IA: American College Testing, Inc., 1995.

Bloom, B. *Taxonomy of Educational Objectives.* Vol. 1: *Cognitive Domain.* New York: McKay, 1956.

Cook, T. D., and Campbell, D. T. *Quasi-Experimentation: Design and Analysis Issues for Field Settings.* Boston: Houghton Mifflin, 1979.

Forrest, A., and Steele, J. M. *Defining and Measuring General Education Knowledge and Skills.* Iowa City, IA: American College Testing, Inc., 1982.

National Center for Educational Statistics. *Digest of Educational Statistics 1995.* U.S. Department of Education Publication No. NCES 95–029. Washington, D.C.: U.S. Government Printing Office, 1995.

Nesler, M. S., Hanner, M. B., Lettus, M. K., and Melburg, V. "External Degree Graduates at Work: Some Empirical Studies." *Proceedings of the National Council of State Boards of Nursing, Inc.* Chicago: National Council of State Boards of Nursing, Inc., 1995, pp. 203–256.

Regents College. *ACT PEP: Regents College Examinations: Test Development and Administration Procedures.* Albany, N.Y.: Regents College, 1995.

Regents College. *Regents College Nursing Catalog.* Albany, N.Y.: Regents College, 1997.

PAULA E. PEINOVICH *is vice president, academic affairs, at Regents College of the University of the State of New York, Albany.*

MITCHELL S. NESLER *is director of research, nursing degree programs, at Regents College of the University of the State of New York, Albany.*

TODD S. THOMAS *is assistant director, institutional research, at Regents College of the University of the State of New York, Albany.*

*The authors discuss a number of adult basic education assessment
strategies at both the individual and program levels, giving attention
to purposes, strengths, and weaknesses.*

Assessment in Adult Basic Education Programs

Eunice N. Askov, Barbara L. Van Horn, Priscilla S. Carman

One teacher confided to the senior author that she never looks at assessment
results because they tell her what she already knows about her learners. Was she
correct, or was she overlooking useful information? How can assessment data be
gathered that will assist all the program stakeholders in decision making?

Assessment in adult basic education (ABE) programs must satisfy multiple stakeholders, each with different purposes for assessment and interests in
the outcomes of the program. Multiple approaches to assessment are necessary
to satisfy these various information needs. For example, in community-based
adult literacy programs usually two stakeholders come to mind: the learner
and the organization (including the instructor). In workplace literacy programs, however, at least two more stakeholders emerge, namely, the union (if
one exists) and the management of the company. Other stakeholders in any
ABE program are the program administrators and the funding agency.

When selecting assessment approaches, three important questions to consider are (1) What are the purposes of assessment? (2) What are the assessment
information needs of each stakeholder? and (3) What are the strengths and
limitations of the various assessment instruments for meeting each of these
needs? While these questions may be raised about any assessment, they
become particularly important in ABE programs that are publicly funded,
where outcomes must be reported in order to receive funding.

The Purposes of Assessment

Assessment of adult students' literacy skills is particularly important because
adults usually come to ABE programs with large gaps in their mastery of skills.
Rarely are individuals equally competent in reading, writing, and math, or in

the subskills that compose these broad areas. Therefore, assessment instruments in ABE programs are used to (1) gather intake information to screen applicants and place them in an instructional program, (2) diagnose each individual's educational strengths and weaknesses in order to develop an instructional plan, (3) measure learner progress to determine individual skill growth, and (4) document the gains of the entire group for program accountability.

Screening. Intake assessments should be conducted in a welcoming and supportive environment. The importance of a successful and reassuring first meeting is well-supported in the research as a key indicator of students' participation in a program. Intake assessment should first involve an interview to determine an individual's reasons for enrolling, goals, interests and talents, and educational history. Screening or placement testing, such as the Test of Adult Basic Education (TABE) Locator Test, the Adult Placement Indicator, or an informal test, is then administered either individually or in a group to provide a starting point for instruction. Lengthy diagnostic or survey tests should be avoided during this first visit.

Diagnosis. Diagnostic testing is conducted when the student is comfortable in the program, usually within the first month of enrollment. This assessment provides more in-depth information about learners' specific skill strengths and weaknesses than the intake assessment. For example, the results of the TABE Complete Battery, the Reading Evaluation Adult Diagnosis (READ), and informal reading inventories provide such diagnostic information. Instructors then use the information to build on students' strengths and to emphasize skill areas that are weak or missing. If the diagnostic tests are standardized, they may also be used for program accountability.

Accountability. Assessments that measure learners' progress are conducted periodically to document the effectiveness of the program for individuals and for the entire group. These assessments are usually standardized but may be informal measures, depending on the stakeholders' needs. It is important, however, that the same assessments that were used for pretesting be used for interim and posttesting. For example, if a student was pretested with a certain level of the TABE and with a locally developed assessment, these same instruments should also be used for measuring gains.

Assessment instruments must meet the needs of all the stakeholders. The teacher described in the first paragraph of this chapter was frustrated because the assessment she administered was selected by someone else for purposes of program accountability instead of for instruction. Assessments should measure what is being taught as well as assisting in documenting program effectiveness and guiding program changes if necessary. The following sections provide information on various assessment instruments and how data are gathered, analyzed, and interpreted to report the learning that is occurring in programs.

Standardized Tests

Standardized tests follow a standard set of directions for test administration, scoring, and interpretation. Learners in different parts of the country, and in different types of programs, should be assessed under the same conditions. A standardized test must be administered and scored and the resulting data interpreted in the same way. If the time limits are ignored, for example, then test norms cannot be used in reporting results. (Ignoring time limits has been justified as "good adult education"; however, it is not appropriate when administering standardized tests.)

Scoring. Although many standardized tests yield a *grade equivalent* score, use of such a score is not recommended for work with adults. Grade equivalent scores do not reflect adults' abilities and may project negative connotations. For example, an adult with a third-grade-equivalent reading level does not behave as a third grader and may be quite competent and skilled in other areas. In fact, the adult's greater background experience may partially compensate for limitations in reading ability.

Recently, standardized adult education tests have been influenced by the National Adult Literacy Survey (NALS), which eliminates grade equivalents. Student scores are arrayed on a proficiency scale of five hundred points forming five levels of competence. Assessment results are reported in terms of both scores and levels, ranging from level one (lowest) to five (highest). The Educational Testing Service (ETS), which created the NALS, also created a commercial version called the ETS Tests of Applied Literacy Skills, which uses the same proficiency scale. Similarly, the Comprehensive Adult Student Assessment System (CASAS) and American College Testing's Work Keys use standard scores instead of grade equivalents. They use scoring scales similar to those used by NALS, thereby eliminating the need for grade equivalents.

Standardized tests have become more contextual in response to the criticism that they measure only generic academic skills. Literacy skills are not easily transferred from one context to another, causing a mismatch when contextual skills are taught, such as in a workplace literacy program, and generic academic skills are assessed. Therefore, the TABE now has a workplace literacy assessment for several occupational clusters. Work Keys is oriented to the workplace, and CASAS has a version to assess basic skills in the workplace. Both Work Keys and CASAS assess workplace literacy skills in general workplace contexts.

Advantages. Standardized tests yield comparable results regardless of location or program type. Therefore, funding agents and policymakers often rely on them for program accountability. Another advantage is that gains on standardized tests may be useful to program administrators and instructors as objective measures of students' progress compared to an external norming group. Standardized tests also may show the group's progress toward meeting specified criteria or competencies.

Disadvantages. A limitation of standardized tests is that they may be irrelevant to what is being taught in the curriculum and classroom. For example, a workplace literacy program that uses the context of the job for basic skills instruction should be careful in using standardized tests because the curriculum may not match the test's content. Standardized tests also may not reflect the actual gains that students make because the test may not be assessing the skills being taught. Conversely, the test may assess the same skills that are taught in the instructional program but in a generic context. Under those conditions, the test may indicate students' ability to transfer what is learned to literacy tasks beyond the workplace. Standardized tests are also limited when the group of students is not comparable to the norming group. For example, a test may be normed on students in general adult basic education programs, but the local students may be nonnative speakers of English, disabled, or institutionalized. In such cases, comparisons to the norming group should be made only cautiously.

Misuses. Standardized and norm-referenced tests are misused when the administrator, proctor, or instructor:

- *Ignores the standardized instructions,* such as by giving students as much time as they want to complete the test. Test conditions are then no longer standard and the results are not comparable to the results obtained by others who have taken the same test.
- *Uses different tests before and after instruction* to measure gains. The same test (or alternative forms of the same test) should be used as pretest and posttest because all tests have different norming groups and standards.
- *Administers standardized tests at fixed times* (say, in the fall and in the spring) regardless of the amount of time individuals have spent in the classroom. Individuals who have been in a program for fifteen hours may therefore be compared to those who have had thirty hours of instruction. (If such scheduling is necessary, students' scores should be sorted and reported according to the number of hours of instruction, such as 0–10, 11–20, 21–30, and so on.)
- *Administers standardized pretests before students feel comfortable in the program.* Students tend to test below their actual capabilities on the pretest and then higher on the posttest, when they are familiar with the instructional setting. The result is that the gains actually due to instruction are not known.
- *Uses an inappropriate level of a standardized test for pretesting and posttesting.* If students take a test that is too difficult, they may score at the "floor" of the test and not show what they know; conversely, if the test is too easy they may score at the "ceiling" and not show any growth over time.
- *Reports only grade-equivalent scores.* Standard scores are more accurate because they account for the inevitable amount of test errors in scores.
- *Compares students' test scores to an inappropriate norming group* (for example, using norms developed on a general population for special needs students). The norming group used by the test developer can be identified by reading the test's technical manual.
- *Averages median or percentile scores for presenting a group's performance.* The only scores that can be legitimately reported as average or mean scores are standard and raw scores. (Raw scores are limited because they do not reflect normative data and cannot be used across test levels.)

Other Types of Assessment

Traditionally, ABE programs have used standardized, norm-referenced achievement tests. Alternatives to norm-referenced achievement tests include criterion-referenced, curriculum-based, performance-based, and informal assessments. Some of these tests are standardized, such as the CASAS; many, however, are informal assessments created by curriculum developers or locally by programs.

Criterion-Referenced Assessments. Criterion-referenced tests (CRTs) measure skill mastery instead of making comparisons to a norming group. The individual's performance is compared to his or her earlier performance in achieving or mastering a particular skill. Instructors find that CRTs are useful for instructional planning in competency-based programs because these assessments indicate whether an individual has mastered a particular skill at a specified level of competence (say, 80 percent). CASAS is perhaps the best-known criterion-referenced literacy assessment in adult education. It is also standardized in that the test administrator is to follow standard administration procedures, but it is not norm-referenced, because an individual's performance is not compared to a norming group.

Curriculum-Based Assessment. Curriculum-based assessment (CBA) involves tests that assess learning from a given set of curriculum materials. Examples are the tests included in the *Challenger* and *Number Power* textbook series (Murphy, 1989; Frechette, 1993). In contrast to criterion-referenced assessment, CBA does not measure skill mastery. Instead it measures whether or not the students have learned what has been taught in the instructional materials. For comparisons to be meaningful, all learners would have to use the same curriculum. The major exception is the General Educational Development (GED) Test, which is a well-established curriculum-based assessment that assesses the skills and knowledge required for high school graduation.

Performance-Based Assessment. Performance-based assessment is a technique for measuring skill applications through demonstrations of competency. Some performance assessments require paper-and-pencil responses; others use computer simulations or real-life demonstrations of competency. As a standardized performance-based assessment, and an alternative to the GED, the National External Diploma Program, or EDP, designed by the American Council on Education, assesses adults' competence acquired through life experiences and self-directed learning. Tests have recently been devised to assess basic skills through computer-based simulations of real problems encountered in a workplace, such as Curriculum Associates' A Day in the Life . . . Assessment. The computer presentation also lends standardization to the assessment procedures.

Performance-based assessments may be particularly useful for nonnative speakers and disabled individuals who may not perform well on paper-and-pencil standardized tests. The EDP, for example, guides adults through a series of activities to document their ability to apply literacy skills in typical adult situations, such as renting an apartment. Standardized, performance-based assessments such as the EDP also may be used for program evaluation and accountability. Learners frequently find this type of assessment meaningful because they can see objective evidence of what they have learned.

Informal Assessment. Program administrators and funders are most interested in generalizable information and in the overall effectiveness of ABE programs. Conversely, adult education instructors and learners are most interested in individual progress. As a result, instructors may reject standardized instruments as inadequate because the tests do not provide sufficient detail about the learners' skills and abilities, making it difficult to plan instruction. Instructors also may believe that standardized tests do not adequately document learner gains.

Efforts to supplement standardized test data often focus on the use of informal assessments. For example, programs might adopt portfolio assessment, teacher-developed checklists, or curriculum-based assessments to assist in collecting additional information about learners' progress. Informal instruments, often developed by program staff, can involve instructors and learners in the assessment process. They can help learners set goals and guide instruction. They can also document changes in a learner's self-esteem or track small steps toward larger goals.

Unfortunately these same assessment activities fall short in meeting requirements for program accountability. Informal instruments are valid within a program; however, the resulting data do not translate across programs. In many instances, little evidence exists that the informal instruments are reliable or even that program staff agree on the purpose or outcomes expected from the assessment. As a result, while informal assessments may be valuable tools in a classroom, they are not replacements for standardized tests.

Informal tests can be commercial, but many are teacher constructed. Instructors and, on occasion, learners working with instructors design informal tests that reflect the skills and knowledge presented in the curriculum, the general instructional/educational goals of the program, or learners' self-selected goals. An instructor may design an informal performance-based assessment to determine learners' ability to perform activities using basic skills and knowledge taught in a customized workplace literacy program (for example, learners may read tables and charts to solve a specific workplace problem). Learners also may select personal goals and, with the instructor, develop milestones to document progress toward the goals. The learner's goal, for example, may be to learn personal money management. Milestones might include learning to perform math operations associated with budgets and developing a family budget.

Tests usually measure a learner's performance at one point in time. Informal assessment tools provide an opportunity to integrate ongoing assessment with the instructional process. Informal assessments can help track progress as learners move toward improved skills.

Informal assessment may involved the following activities:

Observation. Instructors purposefully observe learners as they work, looking for effective use of skills or areas that require additional work. Observations may be recorded in unstructured and open-ended or semistructured anecdotal records or journals. Unstructured records include the instructor's notes about the learner's use of basic skills. Comments may vary depending on, for example, the literacy task or the instructor's knowledge of previous assessment results. Semistructured records might use an observation guide consisting of specific literacy skills that should be observed, and a simple rating of plus (+) or minus (–) to indicate whether the skill was observed and mastered.

Self-Assessments. Instructors should encourage students to reflect on their learning and explore how and why their work shows progress or the need for additional practice. Reflection engages learners in the educational process, demanding that they evaluate their work, think of possible solutions to problems, and become responsible for progress toward and ultimately the achievement of personal goals.

Self-assessments can take various forms, including unstructured interviews, reflective journals, or checklists. Holt (1994) provides several examples of open-ended surveys and questionnaires, which focus on English as a second language (ESL) and family literacy programs but are adaptable to other settings.

Informal Reading Inventories. Informal reading inventories (IRIs) usually consist of a word list and a series of graded reading passages. The word list, read orally, is used as a locator to determine where the learner should begin the reading passages. Each level usually includes two passages, one to be read orally and one to be read silently. The instructor records miscues (such as omitted or inserted words and deleted word endings) observed during oral reading. The instructor then asks several vocabulary and comprehension questions, records the responses, and stops the assessment when the learner misses a specified number of questions. IRIs can be used to diagnose a learner's skill in oral and silent reading comprehension as well as to identify reading miscues. This information can then be used to develop an individual education plan and identify appropriate instructional strategies.

Retell Exercises. Retell exercises require learners to tell what they have read in a selected passage. Although analyzing responses can be difficult, retelling can provide information about learners' text comprehension, use of metacognitive strategies (that is, connections with prior knowledge or generalizations to real-world situations), and facility with language. Herrmann (1994) provides a format for recording learner responses during retelling that provides structure for the instructor to use in scoring the retelling.

Writing Samples. Collected over time, writing samples can serve to document the learner's growth as a writer. Careful analysis of the samples can provide information on specific skills (for example, use of grammar, spelling, and sentence and paragraph structure) and direction for instruction and guided practice. Checklists and criteria are available to evaluate various aspects of adults' writing, such as grammar and expression of ideas. For example, Bear (1987) and MacKillop and Holzman (1990) provide criteria for evaluating writing samples that provide objectivity to the process.

Logs and Checklists. Students can record situations in which they use literacy skills outside the classroom. They record what and how much they read or how much they write, or they record situations in which they applied math principles or used reading skills to solve a practical problem. Over time students include more information as they become accustomed to thinking about the role that literacy plays in their lives. This information can be used to document learners' application of literacy skills in real-world contexts.

Checklists are more structured than logs, making it easier to analyze the information being collected. Existing checklists such as those found in McGrail and Schwartz (1993) and Auerbach (1992) can be used or new ones can be developed to meet specific needs.

Portfolio Assessment. Portfolios may be used for assessment of student learning, including both prior learning and current learning associated with a class, with the latter most commonly found in ABE programs and referred to as performance portfolios. Students demonstrate what they have learned in class by keeping and displaying the best products of their work. Instructors can select from a number of portfolio approaches, ranging from the strictly personal to broad yet systematic collections of student work. Portfolios are not merely work folders, however. They are purposeful collections of work that demonstrate progress or achievement in selected areas of study. Portfolios may be process oriented (that is, writing samples in various stages of completion) or product oriented (that is, finished projects).

Portfolios can focus on one aspect of learners' work or include several areas. They might focus on documenting learners' progress toward developing workplace competencies. For example, adults in a job preparation class may document their ability to be punctual by maintaining a record of their class arrival times; the list can be verified by project staff. Conversely, a portfolio can be very personal, focusing on documenting the impact of program participation on the learner's life. This type of portfolio may have limited value for tracking the learner's progress in developing basic skills. However, it may be invaluable to the individual as visual evidence of the program's value to him or her personally.

While learners assemble the portfolio with assistance from the instructor, an orientation to its purpose, contents, structure, and intended outcomes is important. Although instructors can add work to the portfolio, the primary responsibility lies with the learner. It is therefore important to describe the requirements and expectations for the portfolio assessment before beginning the process, including setting goals or outlining expected outcomes, identifying the types of information to be collected to demonstrate progress, and listing criteria that will be used to evaluate the portfolio contents. As learners add material to the portfolio, they should include brief explanations of why the material is important, thus providing an ongoing record of their thoughts about their work. Finally, instructors should work regularly with learners to review the portfolio and summarize progress toward the selected goals or outcomes.

Providing a Supportive Testing Environment

Test anxiety is common in adult education settings. Adult learners may become visibly uncomfortable when placed in a testing situation. They may sweat or sigh audibly during testing; their hands may shake or they may fidget nervously. Adult educators must provide a comfortable and reassuring testing atmosphere, yet one that yields an accurate picture of the learners' educational achievements, strengths, and weaknesses.

Test anxiety is both a physical and emotional response that may affect a learner's ability to concentrate and perform well on a test. For many adult learners, test anxiety is based on past experiences. They may have a history of repeated failure (either real or perceived) in school. Some ESL students may have had little formal education in their native countries and may be unfamiliar with the testing situation itself. And many adult learners may have never learned specific test-taking strategies to ease their anxieties. Some or all of these factors combine to create an unrealistic perception of the testing situation.

Some programs may not be able to teach test-taking strategies prior to testing due to time constraints. However, all programs can provide a supportive testing environment that will help learners overcome or ease their testing anxieties. The following approaches can be used before, during, and after testing:

- Avoid the word *test*, especially if students seem overly sensitive to the testing situation. For example, one might say, "I'd like you to solve these problems so we can decide what skills to work on. We'll go over the answers together."
- Explain the purpose of the test in clear, simple language. Make sure everyone understands.
- Ask whether students have any anxieties or worries about taking the test. Discuss test anxiety and its symptoms.
- Provide relaxation and positive visualization exercises, such as taking a deep breath. Have learners close their eyes and visualize success.
- Let students ask questions before they begin.
- Allow students to write in the test booklets if they cannot use the answer sheets, or if they have vision or perception problems.
- Watch learners while they are taking the test. Approach anyone who appears upset or frustrated and offer reassuring comments. In severe cases, reschedule the test for another time.
- Allow students to review tests after they are analyzed and discuss the kinds of errors that were made. Schedule private meetings to review individual test results.

Concluding Remarks

For an assessment program to work, all program staff must understand the purposes of assessment and the policies related to administration of various types of assessments. The following recommendations are based on practice:

- *Establish consistent guidelines based on the purposes for assessment.* It is important that all program staff understand these guidelines and comply with them. Program administrators should orient all counseling and instructional staff by reviewing these guidelines to ensure that assessment data are collected in a consistent manner. Staff should be familiar with the assessments used in their program. They should understand and use appropriate procedures for administering standardized and informal tests and for recording data.

- *Involve learners in the assessment process.* Instructors and students should view assessment as part of the learning process. They should meet regularly to discuss assessment results and to plan or revise educational plans. Effective assessment should help learners to identify learning goals and help instructors and learners to plan meaningful instruction.

- *Review testing practices and procedures to evaluate both their appropriateness and effectiveness.* Program planning is an ongoing process. ABE providers should review and evaluate the various components of the program as a process of renewal and improvement. Both internal (for example, staff turnover) and external factors (for example, funding requirements) affect the ability of a program to meet the needs of adult learners. An annual review of policies and procedures is recommended.

Understanding the information needs of the various program stakeholders helps everyone to appreciate the value of different types of assessment. Some assessments are most useful in planning instruction while others yield important data that can be used for program accountability and improvement.

References

Auerbach, E. R. *Making Meaning, Making Change: Participatory Curriculum Development for Adult ESL Literacy.* Washington, D.C.: Center for Applied Linguistics, 1992.

Bear, D. R. *On the Hurricane Deck of a Mule: Teaching Adults to Read Using Language Experience and Oral History Techniques.* Reno, Nev.: Reno Center for Learning and Literacy, 1987. (ED 294 155)

Frechette, E. *Number Power* (series). Chicago: Contemporary Books, 1993.

Herrmann, B. A. (ed.). *The Volunteer Tutor's Toolbox.* Newark, Del.: International Reading Association, 1994.

Holt, D. D. (ed.). *Assessing Success in Family Literacy Projects.* Washington, D.C.: Center for Applied Linguistics, 1994.

MacKillop, J., and Holzman, M. (eds.). *Gateway: Paths to Adult Learning.* Philadelphia: Philip Morris Companies, Inc., 1990.

McGrail, L., and Schwartz, R. (eds.). *Adventures in Assessment: The Tale of the Tools.* Boston: World Education/System for Adult Basic Education Support, 1993.

Murphy, C. *Challenger* (series). Syracuse, N.Y.: New Readers Press, 1989.

EUNICE N. ASKOV is professor of education and director of the Institute for the Study of Adult Literacy at The Pennsylvania State University-University Park.

BARBARA L. VAN HORN is a literacy specialist at the Institute for the Study of Adult Literacy at The Pennsylvania State University-University Park.

PRISCILLA S. CARMAN is a literacy specialist at the Institute for the Study of Adult Literacy at The Pennsylvania State University-University Park.

The use of narratives as assessment tools provides validation for new areas of learning in the workplace.

Assessing Workplace Learning: New Trends and Possibilities

Patricia L. Inman, Sally Vernon

Over the past decade there has been a surge of interest in learning in the workplace. Three interrelated issues have focused attention on the subject. First, the weakening of American competitiveness in the world market has precipitated a reexamination of the structure of the American corporation. Study of other models, particularly the Japanese approach, has resulted in the determination that Japanese success has been due to its engaged and reflective workers. In addition, Japan and other highly competitive countries have emphasized collaboration and continuous learning for workers at all levels of the organization.

Second, the rate of technological innovation has been increasing and as a result more people within organizations have had access to information. Old ideas about skill building and application have given way to a growing realization that the workplace of the future must rely on continuous learning and relearning in order to deal effectively with the increasing technical sophistication of the American workplace.

Third, as a result of the other two trends, the necessity of having a prepared workforce capable of meeting the demands of continuous change has begun to pose real problems for corporations. New concerns have arisen about the basic literacy of the workforce, while the educational level for entering workers has been raised substantially. All of this has led to a reconceptualization of the role of workplace learning and the development of new approaches that focus on experience, reflection, and more nontraditional learning (Watkins, 1995; Wiggenhorn, 1990).

Simultaneously, questions have been raised about how to assess the outcomes of these and other approaches to workplace learning. For example, how do we know if learning is occurring or what skill has been acquired? Have workers achieved the skills or practices that were intended and/or others that were unanticipated? Were the learning outcomes consistent with the expenses incurred and the corporate mission?

Many philosophies and practices come into play in assessing learning in the workplace. How one assesses learning in the workplace depends very much on how one views learning in the workplace. Before assessment of any kind can take place, one must first define workplace learning. This chapter attempts to do that by presenting perspectives on learning in the context of the workplace; by discussing the changing role of individual, group, and organizational learning; and by suggesting some innovative assessment tools.

Overview

As many writers have pointed out, learning in the workplace is not new. In fact, before the nineteenth-century drive to incorporate vocational education into preparatory education, workplace learning was the norm in all fields. Beginning in the early years of the twentieth century, workplace learning became more formalized, with the development of corporate schools and more rationalized approaches to learning (Kett, 1994; Nelson-Rowe, 1991). The period between the World Wars saw growth in industrial training programs, and the beginnings of what would become the field of training. The real spurt in growth occurred after World War II, especially during the 1950s and 1960s. The 1970s and 1980s saw a tremendous expansion of corporate education programs. No longer were these programs considered to be marginal to the corporate mission. In fact, the expansion efforts were driven by the new perspectives on worldwide competition and by the need to improve performance and hence profitability. In addition, changing technologies have changed the dynamics of employment, with greater emphasis on job mobility and the need to constantly upgrade and possibly change technical skills (Watkins, 1995).

As the role of learning in the workplace has changed, so too has the view of what exactly should constitute this learning. Initial efforts focused on technical or specialized skills, but current efforts draw on broader conceptualizations of knowledge and knowing. Assessment of this learning has also broadened as the new techniques have incorporated a more holistic approach. Rather than restricting learning to the smallest component of any task, training and human resource development programs now focus more on contextualized and situated learning that go beyond the task to understand where it fits into both the individual's and the corporation's circumstances.

Victoria Marsick (1987) relates these changing concepts of knowledge to three levels of learning that mirror the changes that have taken place in current thinking about workplace learning and development. She uses the analogy of different lenses—technical, interpretive, and strategic—to help explain these different approaches to workplace learning.

The *technical* paradigm emphasizes mastery of skills and direct applications of knowledge. Assessment usually consists of some variation of pretesting and posttesting to measure what the participant knew before training and what he or she knows now. This approach utilizes scientific models designed to ensure that the corporate world receives the greatest return on its investment. Criteria are preestablished by trainers, and programs are evaluated on the basis of whether these criteria are met. As training has developed as a field, the principal concern has been the development of criteria to measure effectiveness (Marsick, 1987).

The *interpretive* paradigm sees learning as a process of interaction. The role of the instructor is to help learners understand the ways in which learning can take on meaning in their own lives. Assessment approaches include the use of questionnaires and surveys—instruments such as learning-style inventories and individual assessments—that relate life experiences to work situations.

The *strategic* paradigm encourages learners to see learning and corporate needs in a more holistic manner. The ways that social, cultural, historic, and economic forces affect learners and their work situations are critically examined (Marsick, 1987).

Changing Views of Learning in the Workplace

These different paradigms reflect the historical emphases of workplace learning programs. For example, the roots of the technical approach lie in behavioral and cognitive psychology. Initially, training programs assumed that trainees were passive recipients of instructional programs. They utilized didactic methods of instruction such as lectures, training films, transparencies, and case studies. After World War II, instructional design began to include a more active role for trainees, with the introduction of action strategies such as role-plays, games, and simulations. These action strategies went beyond technical approaches in enabling participants to demonstrate how they would utilize the concepts they had acquired in training, and to obtain feedback on their actions. This approach to training was designed to decrease the likelihood that mistakes in learning would be transferred to the work floor (Leatherman, 1990).

By the late 1980s, shifts in corporate structure began as the United States tried to adapt its corporations to greater competition with Japan, Germany, and other countries (Carnevale, 1991). These competitors believed that worker participation, frequently in the form of teams or quality circles, was essential. They promoted this participation in all aspects of the organization, including decision making, production, and training design (Kanter, 1983; Peters, 1987).

This change involved a major paradigm shift. While the post–World War II economic dominance of the American corporation had been built on notions of individualism, autonomy, and competition, the new participative model focused on cooperation and collaboration (Bellah, 1985). This new model involved changing the underlying assumptions regarding individual and team performance at every level of work, and adopting concepts related to action learning, the reflective practitioner, and the consideration of more incidental forms of learning. The purpose of these approaches was to broaden problem-solving abilities and to enable workers to critically reflect on their tasks (Carnevale, Gainer, and Villet, 1990; Catalanello and Redding, 1994; Block, 1993; Marsick, 1987; Mitroff, 1993; Watkins and Marsick, 1993).

Senge (1990) in particular articulated the view that these new approaches—action, informal, and incidental learning—all led to the creation of the "learning organization." According to Senge, becoming a learning organization involves a commitment to learning and change at all levels of the organization. Learning organizations are "organizations where people continually expand their capacity to create the results they truly desire, where new and expansive patterns of thinking are nurtured, where collective aspiration is set free, and where people are continually learning how to learning together" (p. 1).

Senge (1990) identified five elements of the learning organization: personal mastery, systems thinking, mental models, shared vision, and team learning. These elements are all interconnected. Thus learning organizations are based on the connections between *personal mastery* (a special level of proficiency) and *systems thinking* (a conceptual model), which shows patterns of connection. *Mental models* are deeply ingrained assumptions or generalizations that influence action, while *shared vision* is the common organizational identity or sense of destiny. *Team learning* is the way the entire organization or group gains knowledge. Senge feels that these five disciplines must be reflected in productive organizations. In this sense, productive organizations are profitable agencies whose approaches are tempered by societal needs.

Senge's model of the learning organization involves a movement away from prescription and a greater emphasis on the connection between performance and learning. It also lends itself to a greater concern with long-term solutions rather than short-term fixes. Inherent within this view is a reconceptualization of management and leadership (Schein, 1991).

New Approaches to Assessment

As the transformation of training designs and instructional strategies have evolved, so have assessment strategies. Initially, assessment methodology relied on testing the knowledge acquired by trainees during the period of training. Frequently, this testing was associated with management by objectives, with criterion-referenced models, or with competency-based models of training and assessment. With the introduction of more active teaching strategies, the definition of effectiveness was extended to include classroom participation, demonstrations of acquired knowledge such as presentations and simulations, or the development of learning portfolios (Caffarella, 1994).

Senge (1990) states that at the heart of the learning organization is a shift of mind—from seeing ourselves as separate from the world to seeing ourselves as connected to the world. Assessment of such organizational learning consists of helping individuals and groups to see how they can create their own workplace reality. It means extending ideas about what workplace learning is and what knowledge can be utilized within the workplace. The biggest questions deal with how to implement these new ideas within workplace settings. Assessment of workplace learning in today's challenging environment centers on organizational transformation. Senge (1994) suggests that the following areas or organizational systems should undergo review, revision, and continuous assessment: performance management systems, performance feedback systems, reward systems, recruitment systems, development systems, and decision-making systems.

Many of the suggested practices involve real-time group dialogue surrounding organizational change and learning. The purpose of these exercises is to bring to the surface assumptions about the organization and then to derive a new set of assumptions that will formulate new values and ultimately redirect the organization. Rather than being a separate, differentiated task, assessment is embedded in these new practices. The principal concern is the development of measurements that include the perspectives of the individual, the group, and the whole organization, while encouraging continuous, connected learning and reflection. One trend has been to take education and learning outside the classroom, thus reversing the trend of more than fifty years. Learning is now redirected to the work floor and to other work environments. Those who conduct the training become participant observers or coaches who share observations with workers and create work-floor dialogue. The aim is to develop an integrated learning environment that deals with real problems. New approaches include the use of job shadowing, learning coaches, and stewardship (Watkins and Marsick, 1993).

But with these new efforts comes the question of how the organization can determine effectiveness. After all, despite the claims that workplace learning involves the whole person, the ultimate aim is still to increase competitiveness and productivity while simultaneously encouraging innovation and creativity. One of the key innovations in terms of assessment has been a reorientation toward valuing learning that takes place outside of the workplace altogether. This has come about because of a variety of social and demographic changes. As the workplace has become more diverse, and as women in particular have moved into managerial positions, the more traditionally oriented workplace learning programs have been presented with a challenge. Individual assessments of technical knowledge often mitigate or ignore the diverse knowledges that individuals bring to the workplace.

In addition, organizations have recognized that simple technical learning is not sufficient and that a more flexible approach to learning and its assessment needs to be adopted. David Limerick (1990) conducted a study that examined linkages between strategy, structure, and culture in fifty Australian business and government organizations. One of the greatest concerns among these groups (all were deemed successful) was that current assessment tools used in the workplace did not adequately focus on the skills necessary to create effective organizations. "They wanted increased attention focused on programs that help individuals map and understand themselves; stimulate symbolic thinking, intuition, and empathy; encourage the capacity to tolerate ambiguity and paradox; and develop networking and political skills" (p. 63).

While there is recognition that simple quantitative measures do not adequately measure the qualities of what Limerick calls *collaborative individualism,* organizations have been hesitant to move away from these measures because they are so easily understandable, and because they immediately indicate the profitability of any given program.

One of the more promising approaches has been the use of narrative in assessing both new learning and learning that an individual brings to the workplace. Polkinghorne (1988) notes that people in many different settings already work with narratives on an informal basis. "They are concerned with people's stories; they work with case histories and use narrative explanations to understand why the people they work with behave as they do."

Narrative provides a vehicle for examining reality in all of its complexity. It allows for self-reflection and analysis both individually and in groups. At the individual level, narratives help people see who they are and where they are headed. At the group and organizational levels, they serve to give cohesion to shared beliefs in the production of meaning. The knowledge generated increases the power and control that individuals and groups have over their own actions (Howard and Conway, 1986).

Some organizations have begun to experiment with narrative in their assessment procedures. Camcar Textron, in Rockford, Illinois, has developed a personal assessment tool that incorporates elements of narrative (M. West, personal interview with author, June 16, 1997). As part of a larger management development program, career development classes have been designed that ask participants to keep journals that reflect on their lives and to pursue connections between their own experiences and the corporation's goals. Employees write a narrative that reflects on several issues. Reflection plays a key role in developing a personal narrative. Employees examine workplace learning through three lenses: (1) What knowledge do I bring to the workplace? (2) How does this fit into the context of the organization's strategic plan? and (3) What learning project would be most appropriate for my organizational role?

This process presents individual career development in a new perspective. First, it acknowledges that individuals have to perform in their current positions in ways that distinguish them from others. Second, they need to see themselves as lifelong learners so that when opportunities become available they are prepared to take on new assignments. Third, they must have a heightened sense of awareness about themselves and an understanding of human nature. They need to understand their own strengths and weaknesses and to seek continually to improve themselves. Thus assessment takes place at both macro and micro levels as individuals place personal learning agendas within the context of organizational strategic plans.

Drawing on Senge's idea of personal mastery, the Camcar program seeks to help employees look at their accomplishments and connect these to the organization. The skills analyzed include both formal and informal learning experiences from both inside and outside the workplace. The key question is, How does one fit into the organization as a whole? This puts learning into a context somewhat like the act of discovering a new piece to a puzzle. Narratives also facilitate individual discovery of organizational politics and culture (M. West, personal interview with author, 1997).

This reflective process helps employees to decide what they need to learn. In effect, it transfers power for deciding on training from the trainer to the worker. Employees assess their strengths and knowledge through the maintenance of a learning journal. Learning patterns and individual strengths are documented as lists of accomplishment emerge. "The journal can be used in three time dimensions: to capture the present, to reflect on one's life history, and to create the future" (Walden, 1995, p. 19).

Narrative assessments serve as both a process and a product. One of the difficulties is that not all learners know how to conduct self-assessments, particularly through the use of narrative. Taylor (1995) suggests providing questions for reflection when individuals begin learning journals. At Camcar, participants attend a four-day workshop that introduces the concept of narrative assessment and ultimately of a career portfolio that is the result of three narrative assessments. Each of these assessment covers the employee's experiences from a different perspective: current personal mastery, the place of his or her learning within an organizational context, and the development of a learning project and journal. The aim of the career portfolio is to aid workers in becoming more self-directed within an organizational structure and thus to make them responsible for their own learning and its assessment (M. West, personal interview with author, 1997). Besides enhancing skills in self-analysis, narratives can also help individuals to discover common ground within organizations. The development of this common ground helps build consensus and leads to collaborative action (Weisbord, 1992).

The related process of scenario building provides a sense of wholeness while looking at particular narratives within the organization. A scenario—literally a script for a play—is "a tool for ordering one's perceptions about alternative future environments in which decisions might be played out" (Schwartz, 1991, p. 4). Scenario building involves the use of narrative to analyze and understand organizational situations as plots that may be played out. The process involves the development of three or four plots and associated narratives. This type of activity forces individuals not only to reflect on their sense of reality but also to reorganize their perceptions for future growth within the workplace community. Scenarios are used to assess the dynamics of change in the workplace. Just as important, this tool helps individuals to become comfortable with the uncertainty of change.

Preparing a scenario involves an analysis followed by a synthesis of information. The analysis looks at the underlying structure and dynamics of the various forces that are driving change. Typically a distinction is made between two types of driving forces: those that are predetermined and those that are uncertain. Information compiled during the analysis phase of scenario planning is synthesized into a range of plot lines, and then detailed narratives describing possible alternative organizational futures are written for each scenario (Miller, Lynham, Provo, and St. Claire, 1997, p. 82).

Possible changes of direction are assessed through an analysis of these scenarios and their alternatives. Georgantzas and Acar (1995) list three advantages of scenario assessment: (1) it can be rigorous, systematic, and factual; (2) it requires only modest amounts of time and resources (scenarios demand more data and calculations than purely subjective models, but less than statistical and econometric models); and (3) it can provide a direct link between the external environment and corporate strategy by allowing strategy makers to formulate, debate, and appraise the company's situation within the context of its competitive and regulatory environments.

The use of scenarios provides snapshots of the process of collective learning. This allows individuals to assess those forces that both encourage and inhibit learning in the workplace. It also continues the process of giving workers greater power over their work by providing them with the means to analyze and assess their own situations.

Process mapping is another means of generating data for narrative assessment (Hunt, 1996). Developed at General Electric, this approach assesses existing business processes and develops a detailed road map for ongoing change and improvement. After individuals and groups provide scenarios of existing and potential systems, the ensuing dialogue reviews possible scenarios and offers participants opportunities for (1) reflecting on the value of multiple perspectives; (2) participating in the process and product of consensus building as participant observers, thus contributing to the dialogic routine; and 3) contributing to the assessment of the revised systems map.

Argyris, Putman, and McLain Smith (1987) developed and utilized the *left-hand column* technique to accomplish two objectives related to the facilitation of authentic dialogue. This technique requires participants of a group dialogue or narration to divide a piece of paper into two columns. In the right-hand column, participants record their spoken contributions to discussion, and in the left-hand column they record their unspoken comments. The material generated is used to reflect on participants' contradictory perspectives on the ideas generated, the reasons for the silent contributions, the ways in which silent contributions act as barriers to continuous learning and improvement, and strategies to improve current and future dialogue and resulting systems and communication.

Conclusion

The expansion of strategies utilized to foster individual, group, and organizational learning and to assess learning outcomes has paralleled the need to reinvent and reengineer the corporate structure. While the post–World War II period emphasized the acquisition of technical, universalized skills and held up individual autonomy as an ideal, new strategies emphasize collaboration and contextualized knowing. As a result, the face of workplace learning has changed and will continue to do so.

Training programs that occur in classrooms continue to be utilized for specific skill development. However, these programs are increasingly being paired with or supplemented by alternative approaches. The combination of approaches offers a far broader learning spectrum that addresses individual, group, and organizational learning and taps the interrelated needs for continuous improvement in each. Anne Lippitt Rarich (1993) addresses the importance of learning connections in organizational renewal when she states that "individuals who are continually clarifying and deepening their personal vision hold the key to a revitalized organization" (p. 152).

The classic corporate structure featured a hierarchical management system and strictly controlled access to information. Employee training was provided according to diagnosed deficiencies. This methodology served as a barrier to individual and group contributions to organizational improvement. Assessment strategies mirrored training strategies. Documented learning outcomes were limited to those that were prescribed and excluded possible learning outcomes that were incidental. These approaches missed the great variety of learning taking place both inside and outside the workplace. They also dismissed metaphorical and informal learning because these could not be easily quantified. This resulted in a gap in the application of new learning and a loss of potential productivity and profitability.

The development of narratives and dialogic approaches to assessment of workplace learning provides vehicles for the ongoing assessment of knowledge on differing levels. Self-assessment increases individual investment in contributing to group and organizational needs. Scenarios offer snapshots of group and organizational synergy, and narratives assist in fostering authentic communication and identifying organizational options for renewal.

The breadth of workplace learning has been expanded, as have approaches to fostering and assessing this learning. Models exist that link continuous learning to organizational improvement, productivity, and global competitiveness. However, there is a need to continue to introduce and test assessment strategies that provide additional data supporting this link. Researchers and practitioners must build on the proven benefits of continuous learning to continuous improvement in workplace productivity that are documented in current literature. Additional assessment models, conceptual frameworks, and strategies are needed to promote a continued focus on the benefits of individual, group, and organizational learning.

References

Argyris, C., Putman, R., and McLain Smith, D. *Action Science*. San Francisco: Jossey-Bass, 1987.

Bellah, R. N., *Habits of the Heart: Individualism and Commitment in American Life*. New York: HarperCollins, 1985.

Block, P. *Stewardship: Choosing Service over Self-Interest.* San Francisco: Berrett-Koehler, 1993.

Caffarella, R. S. *Planning Programs for Adult Learners: A Practical Guide for Educators, Trainers, and Staff Developers.* San Francisco: Jossey-Bass, 1994.

Carnevale, A. P. *America and the New Economy: How New Competitive Standards Are Radically Changing American Workplaces.* San Francisco: Jossey-Bass, 1991.

Carnevale, A. P., Gainer, L. J., and Villet, J. *Training in America: the Organization and Strategic Role of Training.* San Francisco: Jossey-Bass, 1990.

Catalanello, R., and Redding, J. *Strategic Readiness: The Making of the Learning Organization.* San Francisco: Jossey-Bass, 1994.

Georgantzas, N. C., and Acar, W. *Scenario-Driven Planning: Learning to Manage Strategic Uncertainty.* Westport, Conn.: Quorum/Greenwood, 1995.

Howard, G. S., and Conway, C. G. "Can There Be an Empirical Science of Volitional Action?" *American Psychologist,* 1986, *41,* 1241–1252.

Hunt, V. D. *Process Mapping: How to Reengineer Your Business Process.* New York: Wiley, 1996.

Kanter, R. M. *The Change Masters: Innovations for Productivity in the American Corporation.* New York: Simon & Schuster, 1983.

Kett, J. F. *The Pursuit of Knowledge Under Difficulties: From Self-Improvement to Adult Education in America, 1750–1990.* Stanford, Calif.: Stanford University Press, 1994.

Leatherman, D. *The Training Trilogy.* Amherst, Mass.: Human Resource Development Press, 1990.

Limerick, D. C. "Managers of Meaning: From Bob Gelldof's Band Aid to Australian CEO's." *Organizational Dynamics,* Spring 1990, pp. 60–67.

Marsick, V. "New Paradigms for Learning in the Workplace." In V. Marsick (ed.), *Learning in the Workplace.* London: Croom Helm, 1987.

Miller, R. F., Lynham, S. A., Provo, J., and St. Claire, J. M. "Examination of the Use of Scenarios as Learning and Decision Making Tools for Human Resource Development." In R. Torraco (ed.), *Academy of Human Resource Development Conference Proceedings.* Baton Rouge, La.: Academy of Human Resource Development, 1997.

Mitroff, I. *The Unbounded Mind: Breaking the Chains of Traditional Business Thinking.* New York: Oxford University Press, 1993.

Nelson-Rowe, S. "Corporation Schooling and the Labor Market at General Electric." *History of Education Quarterly,* 1991, *31* (1), 27–46.

Peters, T. *Thriving on Chaos: Handbook for a Management Revolution.* New York: Harper-Collins, 1987.

Polkinghorne, D. E. *Narrative Knowing and the Human Sciences.* Albany: State University of New York Press, 1988.

Rarich, A. L. "Organizational Renewal Through a Hunger for Meaning." In P. Barrentine (ed.), *When the Canary Stops Singing: Women's Perspectives on Transforming Business.* San Francisco: Berrett-Koehler, 1993.

Schein, E. H. *Organizational Culture and Leadership.* San Francisco: Jossey-Bass, 1991.

Schwartz, P. *The Art of the Long View.* New York: Doubleday, 1991.

Senge, P. *The Fifth Discipline: The Art and Practice of the Learning Organization.* New York: Doubleday, 1990.

Senge, P. *The Fifth Discipline Fieldbook.* New York: Doubleday, 1994.

Taylor, K. "Sitting Beside Herself: Self-Assessment and Women's Adult Development." In K. Taylor and C. Marienau (eds), *Learning Environments for Women's Adult Development: Bridges Toward Change.* New Directions for Adult and Continuing Education, no. 65. San Francisco: Jossey-Bass, 1995.

Walden, P. "Journal Writing: A Tool for Women Developing as Knowers." In K. Taylor and C. Marienau (eds.), *Learning Environments for Women's Adult Development: Bridges Toward Change.* New Directions for Adult and Continuing Education, no. 65. San Francisco: Jossey-Bass, 1995.

Watkins, K. E. "Workplace Learning: Changing Times, Changing Practices." In W. F. Spikes (ed.), *Workplace Learning*. New Directions for Adult and Continuing Education, no. 68. San Francisco: Jossey-Bass, 1995.

Watkins, K. E., and Marsick, V. J. *Sculpting the Learning Organization: Lessons in the Art and Science of Systemic Change*. San Francisco: Jossey-Bass, 1993.

Weisbord, M. R. *Discovering Common Ground*. San Francisco: Berrett-Koehler, 1992.

Wiggenhorn, W. "Motorola University: When Training Becomes an Education." In R. Howard (ed.), *The Learning Imperative: Managing People for Continuous Innovation*. Cambridge, Mass.: Harvard Business Review Books, 1990.

PATRICIA L. INMAN is a graduate student in Adult Continuing Education at Northern Illinois University, DeKalb.

SALLY VERNON is president of Vernon and Associates in Chicago.

How you think about assessment may shape findings more than the methods used.

Beyond Transfer of Training: Using Multiple Lenses to Assess Community Education Programs

Judith M. Ottoson

The literature on transfer of training dominates the assessment of adult and continuing education programs. This literature asks an assessment question something like this: Did the skills taught in training move or transfer with fidelity to the job site? It is a perfectly reasonable question to ask when assessing program effects. It is not, however, the *only* question that can be asked. Sometimes participants return from adult education programs with things other than skills—for example, ideas or innovations; they return to places other than work—such as home or community settings; and they do so with varying degrees of fidelity to what they learned and where they live. To explore new directions in assessment, this chapter offers researchers and practitioners a variety of lenses: transfer of training, knowledge utilization, application, diffusion, and implementation. Each comes with its own disciplinary base, assumptions, and key variables to assess program-to-practice links.

 The need for different assessment approaches emerged from a recent evaluation of a national training system sponsored by the Center for Substance Abuse Prevention (CSAP). Training and educational programs were among the strategies used by this federal agency to carry out its prevention mandate. The intent of all short-term programs sponsored by the CSAP Training System

This work was supported in part by the Training and Evaluation Branch, Division of Community Prevention and Training, Center for Substance Abuse Prevention, U.S. Department of Health and Human Services to the Pacific Institute for Research and Evaluation under contract #277–91–2004. This chapter is based in part on the keynote presentation to the 1996 Midwest Research-to-Practice Conference, Lincoln, Nebraska.

(CTS) was that participants would return to local communities and engage their prevention-related learning. The assessment challenge emerged from the diversity of training and educational programs within the CTS. *What* was to be engaged by *whom* and *where* varied across the thirty types of CTS programs, which included those that taught health professionals how to screen patients for substance abuse during regular office visits, those that mobilized members of community partnerships to engage in local prevention efforts, and those that empowered participants from cultural specific groups to prevent substance abuse in culturally sensitive ways. One pair of lenses was inadequate to view the effects of this broad training system. The transfer lens provided sharp focus for finding evidence of the use of skills after the training, but blurred or missed other effects, such as the diffusion or local adaptation of ideas. These effects seemed too interesting to toss and too important to be disparaged as unintended.

To explain these diverse CTS findings, different theoretical understandings of the posteducational experience of participants were sought. These are reviewed here and applied to the CTS assessment as a case study. The use of multiple lenses is in line with the long history of research in adult education on reasons for participation in adult and continuing education programs. If adults start from such different points, does it follow that only one lens should be used to assess program effects? Multiple lenses are also consistent with current efforts in the field of program evaluation to move beyond program objectives as the unchallenged determinant of program effects; rather, theory is used to examine assumptions underlying objectives (Shaddish, Cook, and Leviton, 1991). A program can have crystal clear objectives but be based on such muddied theory that the achievement of those objectives is neither feasible nor desirable. As a result, the program may be judged as unsuccessful when it was the underlying theory that was at fault, not the program. The purpose of offering these different theories, or lenses, is not to suggest that one is inherently better or worse. Rather, the purpose is to provide researchers and practitioners with assessment options.

Transfer of Training

The literature on transfer of training is rooted in industrial psychology and is concerned with the positive or negative influence of prior learning on later learning. Transferability is the ability to move between different jobs or tasks with little or no modification. Influences on transfer include program design, work environment, the nature of what is to be transferred, learning retention, generalization, and maintenance. Variables assessed in the evaluation of transfer include overall task similarity, amount of practice time, stimulus variety, perceived similarity between training and work environments, timing of feedback, number of task steps, incentives, opportunity, social systems, habits, and sense of ownership by learners (Annett and Sparrow, 1985; Baldwin and Ford, 1988).

The research base for transfer literature makes it particularly useful in assessing the accomplishment of something with precision and certainty through practical knowledge and ability. Much of the research on learning principles, as it relates to transfer, was conducted on college students before 1970. The studies examined the immediate retention of relatively straightforward memory and psychomotor-skill tasks. Having been one of these college students, I know that memorizing lists of numbers from a rapidly moving index and transferring them to another index within three minutes is not exactly like returning to work from a short-term continuing education program. The transfer lens is used often in business and industry, the military, and other skill training contexts. In these contexts it matters that the pilot, the surgeon, or the chemical worker transfer skills with fidelity and precision. The lives of passengers, patients, and the public depend on it. Transfer also assumes that the context to which a skill transfers is one that supports or can accommodate the skill.

CTS Case Study: Using a Transfer Lens

In the CTS assessment, the transfer lens was used to look for evidence that the skills that had been taught in the CTS were being used back in the community. It was expected that these skills would be evident in a relatively short time and with few or no changes from how they were taught in the CTS program. We found, for example, health professionals using in their own practice the same assessment tool that was taught in the CTS to screen patients for substance abuse. Members of community partnerships who had participated in another workshop used resource lists provided in training to identify support for projects in their own communities. The transfer-of-training lens proved particularly helpful in finding evidence of skill transfer. Success through this lens meant that what was taught in the CTS looked pretty much the same, if not exactly, as it did in practice.

The transfer lens blurred, however, at other kinds of outcomes. For example, when health professionals were found to use another assessment tool, to have adapted the recommended one, to have asked only one question from the tool, or to have thought about screening but not yet done it, it was not clear how to analyze these findings. Although all of these effects may have been a step forward for participants who had had no involvement with substance abuse prevention before the CTS, they did not count as evidence of success from a transfer perspective. They were not precise, visible, intact, or timely. From a transfer perspective, evidence of a step forward or a change was insufficient evidence of success. Transfer is about a precise change, not just any change.

One of the problems with the transfer lens is the assumption that training participants return to contexts that can support or accommodate new skills. This was not the case for many CTS participants. Many returned to work or community settings that did not welcome their new skills and ideas. For example, some health professionals returned to acute care rather than prevention-oriented settings, some members of community partnerships returned to organizations with differing values on collaboration, and some participants in culturally specific training found that the healing or pride generated by being together dissipated with their solo dispersion into the broader community. The fact that skills and ideas moved to posttraining contexts in pieces, in different formats, or in delayed time is less problematic than the assumption of the wholesale transfer of learning. The transfer lens helped to identify certain kinds of effects, but missed or dismissed others.

Knowledge Utilization

The knowledge utilization lens is rooted in the social sciences. It is concerned with questions about what constitutes the use of knowledge. "The issue of utilization has emerged at the interface between science and government. It has to do with our fundamental assumptions about human rationality, progress, and science applied to the creation of a better world" (Patton, 1978, p. 12). Questions about knowledge utilization emerged among program evaluators in the late 1960s when their good efforts to produce evaluation reports about large-scale social programs seemed more to collect dust than to inform decisions. Unlike some academics who see knowledge creation as good in and of itself, evaluators intend that the knowledge they produce be used. Their questions about what constitutes use of evaluation results is translated here to ask what constitutes use of learning from adult and continuing education programs.

Utilization models can be grouped into three broad categories: empiricist, engineering, and enlightenment (Blumer, 1982). From an educational perspective, the knowledge-driven empiricist model feeds facts to adult learners so that they reach the "best" decisions or take the "right" actions. The engineering model provides evidence and conclusions to help adult learners solve complex problems. It overlaps with the instrumental understanding of use found in the transfer-of-training models. In contrast, the enlightenment model seeks to create the kind of intellectual condition that is supportive of problem solving over time that draws on multiple sources and kinds of knowledge.

Each of these models accepts decision making as evidence of use and, therefore, as potential evidence of success. With varying priority, these models assess a wide range of influences on use, including learner understanding, values, beliefs, and expectations, as well as organizational, political, technical, and cultural factors (Patton, 1978; Weiss with Bucuvalas, 1980). From an assessment perspective, instrumental use is easier to find than enlightenment. Instrumental use is comparatively more immediate, observable, and context specific; enlightenment occurs over time, takes varied forms, and crosses multiple contexts. The enlightenment lens is problematic when the real intent is not to assess learning or change but to claim credit for it with a particular program or teaching technique. Because enlightenment takes a long time and has multiple influences, it shares credit for change. The enlightenment lens can be used to assess change, but not to credit a single cause for the effect.

CTS Case Study: Using a Utilization Lens

"Did they use it?" This turned out to be a rather shallow question to ask about the posteducational experiences of CTS participants. Because the transfer lens adequately covered instrumental use, it was the enlightenment perspective that contributed new insight in the CTS assessment. When viewed through this lens, use is understood more as a hologram than as the mirror image of transfer. Enlightenment suggests a series of questions about use: What counts as use? Does it have to be visible? How much has to be used? By when? How well? Alone or with others? In what context? Towards what end? No matter how well objectives are written (Mager, 1975), educators cannot answer all the preceding questions about use for thousands of participants returning to diverse contexts from a large training system such as the CTS. Enlightenment is about use in a real context, not in an abstract condition.

The enlightenment lens suggested different methodological approaches to assessment. First, it led to personal interviews and open-ended survey questions that sought the meaning of use from participants' perspectives. It proved particularly helpful in assessing programs in which participants were diverse and skills were not central outcomes. Second, it led to proximal indicators of enlightenment, such as awareness, decision making, intent, and reflection, which were assessed on questionnaires or during interviews. Such indicators capture changes in thinking and affect that count as evidence of success from an enlightenment perspective. By recognizing use as a conceptual process, behavioral process, or both, the CTS assessment gained latitude in judging success. Programs could be valued for what people thought or felt differently, not just for what they did differently.

Application

The application lens brings into focus how principles, ideas, or theories interface with what constitutes the practical in different contexts (Ottoson, 1995). Because the practical is the opposite of that which is speculative, theoretical, or ideal, much of the application process involves negotiation between concepts and context. Application is less about the precision of skills than about the artistry of practice. It is less about the wholesale transfer of ideas or skills and more about the goodness of fit between ideas and context. It involves not only the use of existing knowledge but also the creation of new knowledge in context. Application complements the lenses of transfer and utilization. While transfer assesses the accuracy of skill movement and enlightenment assesses change, application looks for evidence of ideas and principles in context.

"In applications, the principles may be filtered through a conceptual sieve originating outside science" (Van Frassen, 1991, p. 324). In the filtering process, it is anticipated that principles and ideas will change as they come into practical contact. It is further anticipated that the context in which these ideas are engaged will change as well. The strong role of context in application led

Weiss and Bucuvalas (1980) to suggest that this process be approached as the "sociology of knowledge application" (p. 23). This approach to application leads with the social consequences of knowledge rather than with the psychological processes of transfer. Assessment based on application must deal with the translation and mutual adaptation of ideas and context over time. It is the tricky stuff of assessment. We are no longer looking for mirror images; we are looking for the essence of an idea.

CTS Case Study: Using an Application Lens

Using the application lens, the CTS assessment focused on the interface between the principles and ideas taught in the CTS and the multiple practice contexts to which participants returned. Ideas to be applied included the principles of prevention, understandings of cultural diversity, or theories of social learning. The contexts to which these would be applied varied by geography, culture, organization, and purpose. Using an application lens, we did not expect that these principles, understandings, and theories would look the same in all contexts.

Evidence of application came through different foci. First, assessment sought evidence of the *mutual* adaptation between CTS ideas and the local context. Unless the adaptation is mutual, ideas or context can be co-opted by the other. For example, screening for substance abuse might involve different questions asked by different workers in settings different from those modeled in training. These differences were evidence that prevention principles had been contextualized to local situations. A second and related focus is the connection between principles taught and actions taken or ideas engaged. Transfer looks for the exact skill; application looks for the essence of the idea or principle. A third focus is the multiple influences on application. Rather than separate the CTS from all other influences, application assessment sought to include the CTS as one among many influences on application. A fourth focus is the creation of new knowledge. In contrast to the knowledge utilization lens, which looks for the instrumental or enlightened use of existing knowledge, application anticipates the creation of new knowledge through the negotiation of concept and context. The knowledge created may emerge from practice and is not limited to knowledge, with a capital K, created through research.

Diffusion

Diffusion is concerned with movement or spread of an innovation over time, through communication channels, and among members of a social system (Rogers, 1995). An innovation is an idea or product that is new to the learner, although not necessarily new in time or in other social systems. An innovation might be a skill (transfer) or idea (knowledge utilization and application), but it might also be a product, such as new technology. Like enlightenment, diffusion looks over time at the movement of an innovation and does not limit its view to immediate effects. It examines the sociological and contextual perspectives of innovation movement and expands the psychological focus of transfer. It draws on communications research and has been broadly applied in many fields. It is particularly relevant to adult and continuing education, not only because of it shared roots in agricultural extension, but also because of the extent to which educational programs are often used to disperse innovations.

From a diffusion perspective, education-related factors to be assessed include conditions prior to the educational program, participant knowledge of the innovation, external persuasion to engage the innovation, the decision to adopt an innovation, implementation, and acceptance or rejection of the innovation (Rogers, 1995). It is only at the implementation stage that the innovation moves from ideas to action, that is, from conceptual to instrumental use. Communication channels link factors in the innovation decision-making process among members in a social system. These channels are essential to moving the innovation across time and context. They provide an important focus when using the diffusion lens, but they are also problematic. Although participants in adult and continuing education may be educated within their own social system—for example, a professional or cultural group—they often leave that social system and return to complex practice environments with multiple social systems. In these environments, webs may be a better metaphor for communication than channels.

CTS Case Study: Using a Diffusion Lens

It was like taking horse blinders off to use the diffusion lens in the CTS assessment. With this lens we could look around and see CTS innovations moving across groups, organizations, and communities. Without this lens, much of the posteducational experience for CTS participants would have been missed. When vision was not restricted to tracing the movement of ideas from here to there—from training to job site—we saw multiple "theres." Whether participants transferred, used, or applied their CTS learning, nearly all (97 percent) shared CTS principles, ideas, information, or innovations with others to some extent, thus diffusing ideas from the CTS through numerous channels, such as the media, personal contact, educational programs, and written materials. Diffusion was initiated by individuals, teams of participants, or organizations. Messages about the prevention of substance abuse reached children, youth, and adults. The diffusion lens enabled an examination of the multiplicative effects of adult and continuing education. It helped to assess the "spreadability" of ideas from the CTS throughout multiple social systems, not just through straightforward transfer from training to work site. The diffusion lens also gave insight into postprogram process or interactions, not just the outcomes that resulted from them.

Implementation

The implementation literature has at its heart a question about "how ideas are manifest in a world of behavior" (Pressman and Wildavsky, 1979). Through the implementation lens, ideas clump as policy. Because policy is necessarily a political process, so too is implementation. Variables for analysis from an implementation perspective include issues of power, access, and resources. A range of disciplines—including sociology, political science, economics, and philosophy—provides insight into the complex process by which policy is transformed into programs and practice. Interest in policy implementation grew in the late 1960s, when it was evident that it took more than a good policy or idea to achieve intended outcomes of social reform. It turns out that it also takes more than good ideas and good intentions to engage learning in the world of practice.

Implementation is that vague area somewhere between idea development and program outcome. It is variously described as a stage, an action, or a process that is chiefly either organizational or political in nature. The metaphors of implementation include an assembly line, mutual adaptation, and evolution. These are not unlike the empiricist, engineering, and enlightenment models encountered with knowledge utilization. Implementation has been analyzed from the top down and bottom up, at macro and micro levels, and as part of larger processes, such as change, diffusion, and policy development (Ottoson, 1984). It has been described as a ubiquitous problem that is the analytic equivalent of original sin (Pressman and Wildavsky, 1979).

Major factors to be assessed in educational programs through an implementation lens include the ideas, the context, and the stakeholders. In the traditional model of implementation, ideas as policy are considered a "real" or finished entity before implementation. During implementation strategies are employed that protect and enforce these preset ideas. This understanding of implementation has led some educational agencies to practitioner-proof materials so that they cannot be changed in practice. The traditional model of implementation is more concerned with compliance than with adaptation. In another understanding of implementation, the resultant model, ideas as policy become real *during* implementation and are nurtured toward that end. This approach leads to practitioner-adapted materials that fit the context and culture of local participants. The resultant model of implementation is more concerned with feasibility than with precision. Similarities can be seen between the traditional model of implementation and transfer of training, as well as between the resultant model of implementation and enlightenment or application. In contrast with the in-depth views of transfer, utilization, and application and the wide view of diffusion, implementation takes the long view, linking ideas, programs, and practice.

CTS Case Study: Using an Implementation Lens

Using the implementation lens, an analysis was done of the links between the policy intent of the CTS and training effects. Although a range of CTS effects could be identified through other lenses, the implementation question was whether these effects had anything to do with federal policies toward substance abuse prevention. The links between policy and practice necessarily involved a political analysis. CTS participants who lacked sufficient authority, resources, or access were disadvantaged in implementation. While they may have understood measures of substance abuse prevention, they lacked the influence to implement this understanding in their practice context. Implementation takes more than a good idea. Assessment from an implementation perspective therefore needs to consider issues of power, access, and structure.

Separate or Simultaneous Assessment?

The differences among assessment approaches in the preceding review suggest that if you have seen one process you have not seen them all. These lenses differ in language, tradition, context, and primary stakeholder. Experts in one approach, such as transfer, may be unfamiliar with similar issues in the knowledge utilization or implementation literatures. Despite the differences, it is difficult not to see the ties that bind these assessment approaches. From all these perspectives, it is clear that process matters. What happens between the end of programs and postprogram effects influences program assessment. "Knowing only that intended effects were not achieved is not instructive for future program planning" (Weiss, 1972, p. 39). Knowing how those effects were achieved is also important. How you think about postprogram actions or interactions affects what you see.

Although *what* is assessed changes with the lens used—skills (transfer), research (knowledge utilization), principles (application), innovations (diffusion), or policy (implementation)—commonalties center around process. All these assessment lenses focus on processes that take place over time; that interface between worlds of different values, priorities, and rewards; that have some intent; that engage multiple stakeholders; and that result in multiple outcomes, intended or otherwise.

All of these processes have their mainstream and sidestream approaches. The mainstream approach is most often rational, seeks immediate effect, and presses to protect the idea. The sidestream eschews the rational for intuition and art, takes the winding road to effect, and responds to variabilities in the context. Within the mainstream and sidestreams lies the tension between fidelity to the idea and flexibility in the context. This tension has implications for how programs are assessed, with fidelity to the ideas of programs or flexibility about the contexts of practice.

Rather than always grabbing the same pair of assessment lenses (transfer) to view educational program effects, it is important to have some options. Different lenses can be matched to assessment intent and circumstances, such as the brilliance of enlightenment (sunglasses), the complex interface of application (magnifying glass), the breadth of diffusion (panoramic lens), and the long view of implementation (telescope). In the CTS case study, these multiple lenses enable us to see the transfer of skills, the conceptual changes of enlightenment, the mutual adaptation between ideas and context in application, the spread of ideas in diffusion, and the links between federal policies and training outcomes. Taken together, these multiple approaches to assessment offer a view of program effects that is rich in texture, depth, and composition. They also offer different views of how value is ascribed to programs.

References

Annett, J., and Sparrow, J. "Transfer of Training: A Review of Research and Practical Implications." *Journal of School Health,* 1985, 22 (2), 116–124.

Baldwin, T. T., and Ford, J. K. "Transfer of Training: A Review and Directions for Future Research." *Personnel Psychology,* 1988, 41, 63–105.

Blumer, M. *The Use of Social Research.* Boston: Allen & Unwin, 1982.

Mager, R. F. *Preparing Instructional Objectives.* (2nd ed.) Belmont, Calif.: Fearon, 1975.

Ottoson, J. M. "Reconciling Concept and Context: The Practitioner's Dilemma in Implementing Policy." Unpublished doctoral dissertation, Graduate School of Education, Harvard University, 1984.

Ottoson, J. M. "Reclaiming the Concept of Application: From Social to Technological Process and Back Again." *Adult Education Quarterly,* 1995, 46, 1–30.

Patton, M. Q. *Utilization-Focused Evaluation.* Thousand Oaks, Calif.: Sage, 1978.

Pressman, J. L., and Wildavsky, A. *Implementation.* (2nd ed.) Berkeley, Calif.: University of California Press, 1979.

Rogers, E. M. *Diffusion of Innovations.* (4th ed.) New York: Free Press, 1995.

Shaddish, W. R., Cook, T. D., and Leviton, L. C. *Foundations of Program Evaluation.* Thousand Oaks, Calif.: Sage, 1991.

Van Frassen, B. "The Pragmatics of Explanation." In R. Boyd, P. Gasper, and J. D. Trout (eds.). *The Philosophy of Science.* Cambridge, Mass.: MIT Press, 1991.

Weiss, C. H. *Evaluation Research.* New York: Prentice-Hall, 1972.

Weiss, C. H., with Bucuvalas, M. J. *Social Science Research and Decision Making.* New York: Columbia University Press, 1980.

JUDITH M. OTTOSON *is associate professor in the Department of Educational Studies, Adult Education Program, at the University of British Columbia.*

The basic themes are reviewed and the implications for future practice
are discussed.

Assessment Themes and Issues

Amy D. Rose, Meredyth A. Leahy

Assessment has become inextricably linked to educational discussions of good practice. At its simplest level assessment deals with the central question of whether learning has taken place in a particular setting. We assess in this manner for two principal reasons: to ascertain program effectiveness, and to learn about what the participants have gained and identify the gaps in their knowledge. The first step in such a process of assessment has often involved some kind of pretest and posttest. Yet as the chapters in this volume make clear, what should seemingly be an easy problem of comparison is really much more complex. Simply seeing a change between test results does not give a true gauge of what individuals, particularly adults, have learned. Hence, in recent years those concerned with the assessment of adult learning have focused on several important aspects that go beyond testing.

Beyond Testing

In discussing assessment, it may be useful to distinguish between assessment and evaluation. According to Moran (1997), evaluation is used to make a judgment about how well an individual or group has done in reaching a particular goal. Assessment, conversely, describes learner achievement. Yet despite this seemingly clear distinction, the terms easily overlap and in fact are often used interchangeably. In effect, learner achievement is often a key aspect of the evaluation process and so the two are inextricably related. As program planners have reconceptualized the learning experience, they have reconfigured the assessment process as well. Whereas once assessment was perceived as a fairly mundane effort, there is now fairly widespread recognition of the complexities involved. Assessment is not a static process but one of fundamental change and innovation.

In Chapter One, Kasworm and Marienau develop a set of principles for the assessment of adult learning that are consistent with the generally accepted premises of adult learning. Thus assessment practices need to recognize multiple sources of knowing and the different domains of learning, they need to focus on the active involvement of adults in both the learning and assessment process, they must embrace adult learners' involvement in the broader world, and they must accommodate the wide differentiation among adult learners as they engage in the learning process.

If the process of assessment is to be truly contextualized, it must take into account the individual issues that affect learning and outcomes. As Stephen Brookfield indicates in Chapter Two, the need for reflection and self-assessment sometimes collides with the new demands by external monitors to demonstrate learning and change. This is especially problematic when the learning taking place is not incremental or instrumental but rather involves a different way of thinking or relating to the world.

Innovation in Assessment

One of the more interesting questions deals with the dilemma of how to incorporate innovation into the assessment process. For the moment, the principal thrust of those writing on the topic seems to be the issue of context. In Chapter Four, however, Michelson indicates the potential pitfalls that seemingly revolutionary approaches can undergo as they are integrated into mainstream educational institutions.

Within higher education the entire issue of outcomes assessment illustrates this point. Beginning with the progressive educators of the early twentieth century, there has been a consistent concern with moving education beyond the confining institutional framework of schooling. In particular, this emerged as a concern about what students know rather than about where they learned it. Ralph Tyler, whose work in curriculum theory was pivotal in creating generations of teachers who translated their goals into behavioral objectives, was deeply concerned that such work needed to push teachers toward greater concern with what has actually been taught. Tyler himself was intimately connected to the development during World War II of the General Educational Development exams, which were eventually made available to civilians for use in the granting of equivalency degrees. For Tyler, these exams had two purposes: (1) to expedite the educational travails of returning veterans, and (2) to show that individuals could gain equivalent learning in a wide variety of settings. Tyler saw this issue of equivalency as central to rethinking the entire educational system to focus on learning (or in today's parlance, on outcomes) rather than on time spent in the classroom (Rose, 1990).

The PONSI model (Chapter Three) and the Regents College model (Chapter Five) are both drawn from this early insistence that the emphasis of education should be on the learning, not on the time spent inside a classroom. The question in both of these models, as discussed in Chapter Four, is how to translate experience and the knowledge gained from it into creditable learning. The PONSI model answers this question by evaluating the experience rather than the learner. Admitting that learners take away highly distinct and individualized bodies of knowledge from any one learning experience, PONSI assesses the entire experience in terms of recommended credit.

Portfolio assessment (discussed in Chapter Four) is an almost opposite approach. Recognizing that individuals engage in learning tasks in different ways, the preparation of the portfolio allows learners to indicate exactly what they have learned from a plethora of sources.

Regents College advocates the use of a multifaceted approach, utilizing the combination of testing, portfolio assessment, formal coursework, and the work of assessment agencies such as National PONSI and ACE's CREDIT into a coherent and acceptable degree program.

As Michelson also points out in Chapter Four, the tensions between the attempts to broaden the focus on learning while concurrently seeking academic acceptance can overwhelm educational reform. Rather than redefining the central issues or remaining on the cutting edge of educational reform, these efforts have all too often tried to please the most traditional strongholds on campus. The result has been that too often the promise of reform gives way to a less than innovative reality, especially in terms of educational content. At the root of this issue is really the central question of what knowledge is, who defines it, and how this definition is acted upon within higher education.

Bias or the Issue of Objectivity

Central to the whole question of knowledge is the underlying concern with bias in the assessment of learning. Michelson, in Chapter Four, and Askov, Van Horn, and Carman, in Chapter Six, indicate that too little attention has been paid to the problems of cultural bias that permeate the assessment process. These can manifest as simply the informal assessments of instructors asking questions in a milieu where questions are considered insulting, or as the equally complex but less easily solved issue of admitting to culturally determined notions of learning and what is acceptable learning.

Assessment as an End or as an Integrated Part of Program Delivery

A consistent theme throughout these chapters has been concern with the sectioning off of assessment as a tool to help the teacher gauge learning instead of as a means for helping learners to reflect on their own experiences and their own learning. The premises of adult learning discussed in Chapter One form an interesting basis for examining how assessment is part of the continuous learning loop. This is particularly apparent in the work being done in the learning organization (Chapter Seven), where assessment leads to reflection and further learning. Beyond the issues of formative and summative evaluation, assessment is becoming an integrated part of the actual process of learning.

How Do We Know That a Learner Has Really Learned and Can Utilize This Learning?

There are two aspects to assessing the learning of adults. One focuses on the assessment of what they already know and the other examines how adults have learned and can utilize new learning. Judith Ottoson proposes in Chapter Eight the use of multiple lenses to ascertain how adults transfer their learning from one context (the classroom) to another (the workplace or other real life setting). In enumerating the different ways that transfer can be understood, Ottoson attempts to change our way of thinking about the uses of learning, as well as reminding us of the need to remember contextual factors when assessing transfer.

Conclusion

Assessment and program evaluation are swiftly becoming the bywords of the American educational system today. They are invoked as means of quality assurance and of ensuring that programs are effective. Yet, interestingly, the chief issues within assessment seem to be the interlocking forces that shape each individual's experience of education and learning. Thus there is a simultaneous drive to assess learning that has taken place in many dimensions and that can be utilized in many other dimensions. The tensions arise when the needs of accrediting agencies clash with the needs and understanding of the individual learners. Concomitantly there is a strong desire to understand the ways that adults shape their own learning experiences and how this has an impact on both the learning and utilization of new knowledge. While issues relating to assessment have a long history in all aspects of education, the new focus represents a renewed effort to attend to the actual experience of the learner rather than to the requirements of the school. It remains to be seen whether this promise will be carried out.

References

Moran, J. J. *Assessing Adult Learning: A Guide for Practitioners.* Malabar, Fla.: Krieger, 1997.
Rose, A. D. "Preparing for Veterans: Higher Education and the Efforts to Accredit the Learning of World War II Servicemen and Women." *Adult Education Quarterly,* 1990, 42 (1), 30–45.

AMY D. ROSE is associate professor of Adult Continuing Education at Northern Illinois University, DeKalb.

MEREDYTH A. LEAHY is dean of liberal arts at Regents College of the University of the State of New York, Albany.

INDEX

Ordering Information

New Directions for Adult and Continuing Education is a series of paperback books that explores issues of common interest to instructors, administrators, counselors, and policy makers in a broad range of adult and continuing education settings—such as colleges and universities, extension programs, businesses, the military, prisons, libraries, and museums. Books in the series are published quarterly in Spring, Summer, Fall, and Winter and are available for purchase by subscription and individually.

Subscriptions cost $54.00 for individuals (a savings of 35 percent over single-copy prices) and $90.00 for institutions, agencies, and libraries. Standing orders are accepted. New York residents, add local sales tax for subscriptions. (For subscriptions outside the United States, add $7.00 for shipping via surface mail or $25.00 for air mail. Orders must be prepaid in U.S. dollars by check drawn on a U.S. bank or charged to VISA, MasterCard, or American Express.)

Single copies cost $22.00 plus shipping (see below) when payment accompanies order. California, New Jersey, New York, and Washington, D.C., residents, please include appropriate sales tax. Canadian residents, add GST and any local taxes. Billed orders will be charged shipping and handling. No billed shipments to post office boxes. (Orders from outside the United States must be prepaid in U.S. dollars by check drawn on a U.S. bank or charged to VISA, MasterCard, or American Express.)

Shipping (Single Copies Only): $30.00 and under, add $5.50; to $50.00, add $6.50; to $75.00, add $7.50; to $100.00, add $9.00; to $150.00, add $10.00.

All prices are subject to change.

Discounts for quantity orders are available. Please write to the address below for information.

All orders must include either the name of an individual or an official purchase order number. Please submit your order as follows:
    Subscriptions: specify series and year subscription is to begin
    Single copies: include individual title code (such as ACE 59)

Mail all orders to:
Jossey-Bass Publishers
350 Sansome Street
San Francisco, CA 94104–1342

Phone subscriptions or single-copy orders toll-free at (888) 378–2537 or at (415) 433–1767 (toll call).
Fax orders toll-free to: (800) 605–2665.

For subscription sales outside of the United States, contact any international subscription agency or Jossey-Bass directly.